目　錄

長江三峽

THE THREE
GORGES ON
THE YANGTZE RIVER

海風出版社
HAIFENG PUBLISHING HOUSE

前 言 FOREWORD

三峽，是萬里長江一段山水壯麗的大峽谷，爲中國十大風景名勝之一。它西起四川省奉節縣的白帝城，東至湖北省宜昌市的南津關，由瞿塘峽、巫峽、西陵峽組成，全長192公里。它是長江風光的精華，神州山水中的瑰寶，古往今來，閃耀着迷人的光彩。

長江三峽，無限風光。瞿塘峽的雄偉，巫峽的秀麗，西陵峽的險峻，還有三段峽谷中的大寧河、香溪、神農溪的神奇與古樸，使這馳名世界的山水畫廊氣象萬千——這裏的羣峰，重岩叠嶂，峭壁對峙，烟籠霧鎖；這裏的江水，洶湧奔騰，驚濤裂岸，百折不回；這裏的奇石，嶙峋崢嶸，千姿百態，似人若物；這裏的溶洞，奇形怪狀，空曠深邃，神秘莫測……三峽的一山一水，一景一物，無不如詩如畫，並伴隨着許多美麗的神話和動人的傳說，令人心馳神往。

長江三峽，地靈人傑。這裏，是中國古文化的發源地之一，著名的大溪文化，在歷史的長河中閃爍着奇光異彩；這裏，孕育了中國偉大的愛國詩人屈原和千古才女王昭君；青山碧水，曾留下李白、杜甫、白居易、劉禹錫、范成大、歐陽修、蘇軾、陸游等詩聖文豪的足跡，留下了許多千古傳頌的詩章；大峽深谷，曾是三國古戰場，是無數英雄豪傑馳騁用武之地；這裏還有許多著名的名勝古跡，白帝城、黃陵廟、南津關……它們同旖旎的山水風光交相輝映，名揚四海。

長江三峽，風情絢麗。奉節的人日踏磧，如一幅優美的風俗畫；秭歸的龍舟賽，似一首磅礴的交響樂；沿着江邊一級級石階，可到巴東去欣賞那奇特的背簍世界，順着彎彎的山路，可到土家人家中參加那別有情趣的婚禮…

青澈碧透的香溪中，那隨桃花開而來，又伴桃花落而去的
桃花魚，將使人眼界大開; 奔湧不息的江流裏，那神態威
武的中華鱘，會令人讚嘆不已; 兩岸那些青青的柑桔園，
正飄出誘人的芬芳……

朋友，投進長江三峽熱情的懷抱吧，在這神奇而美
妙的山水世界中，作一次風光之旅、文化之旅、風情之
旅。這裏的一切，會令你終生難忘！

The Yangtze Gorges is a great valley with a most
splendid landscape on the Yangtze (Changjiang) River and
it is one of the ten most famous scenic sites of China. It
extends from White King Town in Fengjie County,
Sichuan Province to Nanjinguan Pass in Yichang, Hubei
Province, consisting of Qutang Gorge, Wu Gorge and
Xiling Gorge, with a full length of 192 km. It converges
the essence of the scenery on the Yangtze River. As a rar-
ity of landscape of China, it has been displaying its special
charms for thousands of years.

The Yangtze Gorges presents a scene of boundless variety with the magnificence of Qutang Gorge, the elegance
of Wu Gorge, the perilousness of Xiling Gorge as well as
the primitive simplicity and the mysteriousness of the
Daning River, Xiangxi River and Shennong River, which
flow into the great valley. The whole landscape is so kaleidoscopic: the peaks tower into the sky, the steep cliffs facing one another with mists and clouds shrouding them all
the year round; the river rolls forward with swashing
waves beating on the shore; the jagged rocks are of
grotesque shapes; the karst caves are unfathomably deep
and fantastic in shape. . . It is picturesque everywhere, and
what's more, each scene is related to a wonderful fairy
tale or a moving legend which will kindle your meditation
on the remote past.

The beautiful landscape of the gorge region has given
birth to a splendid culture. It is one of the birthplaces of
the civilizations of China. The famous Daxi Culture,
which originated here, has shed brilliant light on the civilizations in the long history. It was here that Qu Yuan, the
earliest Chinese patriotic poet, and Wang Zhaojun, an out-
standing talented woman, were born and brought up. It
was also here that Li Bai, Du Fu, Bai Juyi, Liu Yuxi,
Fan Chengda, Ouyang Xiu, Su Shi, Lu You and other poets and men of letters travelled and left their immortal poems behind. The valleys were once the battlefields during
the period of the Three Kingdoms, where countless heroes
displayed their prowess and talent. Besides, a great many
well-known historical sites, such as White King Town,
Huangling Temple and Nanjinguan Pass, add charm to the
landscape.

The folkways of the gorge region are colourful. The
Commemoration of the Eight-Element Battle Formation
on the seventh day of the first moon is like an exquisite
painting depicting the folkways of the local people. The
dragon boat race in Zigui sounds like a thundering symphony. The stone steps beside the river will lead you to
Badong, where you will find yourself in a world of baskets
carried on the back and the winding path will take you to
a family of Tujia nationality where you may be invited to
a wedding ceremony full of distinctive flavour. . .

The gorge region is also rich in natural resources.
Minnows come to the Xiangxi River when the peach trees
are in full bloom and leave when the blossoms are falling;
Chinese sturgeons with a fierce bearing swim freely in the
Yangtze River; green tangerine orchards deliver captivat-
ing fragrance. . .

You are welcome to the Yangtze Gorges to enjoy the
charming landscape and splendid culture as well as the
colourful folkways. You are sure to be intoxicated with
everything here.

縱將萬管玲瓏筆
難寫瞿塘兩岸山

　　瞿塘峽西起白帝城，東到大溪鎮。峽長雖然祇有8公里，順流而下，瞬間即過，但却有"西控巴渝收萬壑，東連荊楚壓羣山"的雄偉氣勢。兩岸懸崖絕壁，羣峰對峙，赤甲山巍峨江北，白鹽山聳立南岸，山勢岌岌欲墜，峰巒幾乎相接。每當晴空麗日，遠眺赤甲、白鹽，一如仙桃凌空，一如鹽堆萬仞，兩山雲遊霧繞，時隱時現，乃為瞿塘一奇觀。峽中江面最寬處一二百米，最窄處不過幾十米。入峽處兩山陡峭，絕壁相對，猶如雄偉的兩扇大門，鎮一江怒水，控川鄂咽喉，形勢非常險要。正如唐代詩人杜甫所描寫的那樣："衆水會涪萬，瞿塘爭一門"，故有"夔門天下雄"之讚。

　　"若言風景異，三峽此為魁"。當你乘船經其間，仰望千丈峰巒，祇見雲天一綫，奇峰異石，千姿百態。俯視峽江，驚濤雷鳴，一瀉千里，猶如萬馬奔騰，勢不可擋。遊人至此，眞有"峰與天關接，舟從地窟行"之感。

　　瞿塘峽不僅雄偉壯觀，而且名勝古跡衆多。這裏有雲集各朝代書法精品的碑刻；有三峽第一古跡白帝城和孔明巧佈的八陣圖；有傳說奇特的孟良梯；有難解之謎風箱峽和充滿神話色彩的錯開峽。

QUTANG GORGE

　　Qutang Gorge extends eastward from White King Town to Daxi Town. Although the gorge is no more than eight kilometers long and a downstream voyage is only a wink, it has a momentum of controlling the waters from Sichuan on the west and dominating the mountains of Hubei on the east. The river is flanked with steep cliffs and towering peaks. Mt. Chijia on the north and Mt. Baiyan on the south penetrate into the sky, facing each other closely with the crags almost touching in the mid-air, dangerous and tottering. Looking from a distance in a fine day, one sees the former resemble a huge pink peach and the latter a huge heap of white salt glittering all the time. The two mountains disappear in the mist and cloud every now and then. That is the most spectacular scene of the Yangtze Gorges. The widest spot of the river is about two hundred metres and the most narrow spot is only tens of metres. At Kuimen, the entrance of the gorge, the steep cliffs on either side look like two gigantic door leaves closing in on the roaring river and holding the strategic pass between Sichuan and Hubei, perilous in every way. As is depicted in the lines of Du Fu, a poet of the Tang Dynasty: *"All the rivers converge at Fuwan, breaking a way through the rocks at Qutang"*. Kuimen has been marvelled at as "the most dangerous pass of the world".

　　If the landscape of the Yangtze Gorges is a wonder, Qutang Gorge is the wonder of wonders. When you travel through the gorge in a boat and look up at the towering peaks, you see thousands of grotesque crags darkening the daylight with only a narrow opening overhead and the thundering river rolling by vigorously, just like thousands of horses galloping ahead irresistibly. You can't help marvelling at the scene and wondering whether you are sailing to the hell.

　　Qutang Gorge boasts not only splendid sights but also places of historical interest. Concentrated here are the masterworks of calligraphy and stone engravings of different dynasties. There are in the region such historical or legendary sites as White King Town, which is the most ancient town in the Three Gorges, the former site of the Eight-Element Battle Formation designed by Zhuge Liang during the period of the Three Kingdoms, Meng Liang Ladder, which is legendary, and Fengxiang Crevices and Cuokai Gorge, which were wrapped in mystery for thousands of years.

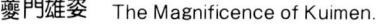

夔門雄姿　The Magnificence of Kuimen.

曦
Morning glow.

夔峽出口處
Exit of Kui
Gorge.

瞿塘峡 Qutang Gorge

"峰與天關接，舟從地窟行。"

"Peaks towering into the sky and boats sailir
through the hell ."

夔門秋月　　Autumn moon beyond Kuimen.

古城奉節

奉節，是三峽西端第一座城市，扼守瞿塘峽西口。奉節原名魚腹縣，爲春秋時期的夔國，是一座有着兩千多年歷史的古城。古城週長3公里，設有五座城門，每座城門都有題額，東門爲"瞿塘天險"，西門爲"全蜀咽喉"，大南門爲"縱目"，小南門爲"觀瀾"，北門爲"肅威"。這些題額都與城門外的風光相關，由此可想象當年的壯麗景色。現在祇剩下大小城門兩座。

大南門是奉節的大門，名爲"依斗門"，取自杜甫的"夔府孤城落日斜，每依南斗望京華"詩句。依斗門高出江面數百級石階，下船後拾級而上，登高遠眺，夔峽風光盡收眼底。

昔日奉節"肩挑背馱行路難，三步一打杵，五步一長嘆"。今日奉節水陸交通發達，工農業發展飛快。這裏盛產黃花、夔柚、柑桔、香桃、枇杷。每臨秋末，柑黃桔紅遍佈街頭，把奉節古城裝點得分外妖嬈。

奉節古城內外還有許多名勝古跡，如唐代詩人杜甫住過的草堂寺，劉備托孤的永安宮遺址等。古人曾經把奉節風光歸納爲"十二景"，如"白帝層巒"、"白鹽曙色"、"峽門秋月"、"文峰瑞彩"等，山水日月渾然一體，引人入勝。其中尤爲出名的，是位於城東梅溪河入江處的諸葛亮八陣圖。這裏是一片沙灘，佈滿大大小小的石頭，可傳說它們能千變萬化，神鬼難測，諸葛亮用它擺下戰陣，曾幾乎困死東吳大將陸遜，嚇退了他帶領的百萬大軍。

FENGJIE，AN ANCIENT CITY

Fengjie，the first city at the western end of the Yangtze Gorges，is situated on the western entrance of Qutang Gorge. Fengjie was fomerly called Yufu County, which was the seat of Kui State during the Spring and Autumn Period. It is a city with a history of more than two thousand years. The ancient walled city has a circumference of three kilometres with five city gates, each with an inscription on it. The inscription on the eastern gate reads: " Natural Barrier of Qutang", the western gate " Throat of Sichuan", the larger southern gate: "Looking Far and Wide", the smaller southern gate : "Viewing Waves", and the northern gate: "Solemn and Mighty". All these inscriptions are related to the surrounding scenes. From the inscriptions we may imagine how spectacular the sights were in the past. At present, however, only two of the city gates are extant.

The larger southern gate is the entrance of Fengjie. It was named Yidou Gate after the lines of Du Fu: *The sun is setting behind the isolated city of Kui State, I am looking to the capital at Yidou by the southern gate*. Yidou Gate is several hundred steps up the river. From here the tourists may feast their eyes on the landscape of Kuimen.

In the past Fengjie's transportation was so poor that people had to carry things by shoulder or back faltering along the narrow paths. Both land and water communications have been greatly developed by now. The development of the communications has made it possible for the agriculture and industry to grow rapidly. Fengjie abounds in day lily, shaddock, tangerine, orange, peach and loquat. In the late autumn the ancient city is decorated with yellow tangerines and red oranges.

In and out of the walled city there are a number of historical sites. Among them are the Thatched Cottage Temple, where Du Fu, a poet of the Tang Dynasty, once lived, and the former site of Yongan Palace, where Liu Bei, the king of Shu Kingdom, entrusted his son to Zhuge Liang, the prime minister. The ancient people divided the landscape of Fengjie into twelve particular scenes such as "the Distant Peaks Around White King Town", "Mt. Baiyan in the Morning Sunlight", "Autumn Moon Beyond Kuimen", "Beautiful Colour of Wenfeng Peak", etc. The mountains and rivers and the sun and the moon come into an integral whole, changing in a fascinating way. Of the kaleidoscopic scenes, the most distinctive is the former site of the Eight-Element Battle Formation designed by Zhuge Liang. The site lies at the mouth of the Meixi River in the east of the city. It is a vast expanse of sandy beach with stones of different sizes scattered all over. The scene changes with the rising and falling of the river. It was said that Zhuge Liang took the topographical advantage and set his Eight-Element Battle Formation here on the beach, which almost bottled up Lu Xun, a general of Wu Kingdom, and thousands of his soldiers.

川東古城奉節　Fengjie, an ancient city in east Sichuan.

鎖江鐵柱，在夔門北岸草堂河口處的石盤上，有兩根鐵柱，各高6.4尺，為宋代末年所置，當枯水時才露出水面，是古代攔江守關的鐵索柱。

River-Locking Iron Post: On the rock at the gorge entrance near The Thatched Temple at Kuimen north of the river stand two iron posts 2.13m tall, set in the late Song Dynasty for chaining defence boats. They emerge only when the river goes down.

"水八陣"

The site of Zhuge Liang's Battle Formation.

白帝城

白帝城，又名白帝廟，像一座孤山兀立於瞿塘峽口，面朝夔門，下臨大江，是三峽最負盛名的名勝古跡。

西漢末年公孫述據蜀，在山上築城，因城中一井冒白氣，宛如白龍，就自稱白帝，並命名此城為白帝城。

白帝城是劉備托孤的地方。蜀漢章武二年，蜀國皇帝劉備伐吳兵敗，退守白帝城。劉備臨死前，將幼子劉禪和國家大事托與丞相諸葛亮。白帝城與三國結下了不解之緣，那屋脊上和飛檐旁一幅幅彩色圖畫，每一幅都是一個生動的三國故事。白帝城內輝煌的古建築中，明良殿內有劉備、諸葛亮、關羽、張飛塑像；武侯祠內有諸葛亮祖孫三代像，個個神采奕奕，栩栩如生。

白帝城是三峽文物薈萃之地，這裏雲集了隋、元、明、清各朝代碑刻74塊，詩文、楹聯、繪畫和書法作品，琳瑯滿目。我國歷代許多大詩人如李白、杜甫、白居易、劉禹錫、蘇軾、黃庭堅、范成大、陸游等，都曾旅居此地，給白帝城留下了許多膾炙人口的詩文。白帝城內，還收藏了不同朝代數以千計的文物，其中有新石器時代的石斧、石箭；奴隸社會的巴式劍、銅斧；戰國時的銅編鐘；秦漢的銅鑒；蜀漢的青瓷虎子；唐代的白瓷畫盒；宋代的描金碗……等等，它們都可作為歷史的導遊，帶你走進三峽古文化的燦爛畫廊。

1 俯瞰白帝城
Bird's-eye view of White King Town.

2 白帝廟
White King Temple.

3 諸葛亮觀星亭
Zhuge Liang's Astrology Pavilion.

4 劉備托孤羣像
Statue group—Liu Bei entrusting his son.

WHITE KING TOWN

White King Town, also called White King Temple, is a walled town over the entrance of Qutang Gorge, facing Kuimen. It is the most famous historical site of the Three Gorges.

Towards the end of the Western Han Dynasty, Gongsun Shu built a walled town on the mountain before he occupied Shu, the present-day Sichuan Province. And as a well in the town often gave off white steam shaped like a white dragon, Gongsun Shu called himself White King and named the town White King Town so as to match the white dragon.

It was in White King Town that Liu Bei, the king of Shu, entrusted his son to his prime minister. In the second year of his reign, Liu Bei attacked Wu and was completely defeated. He retreated to White King Town in despair and bad health. Just before he died he entrusted his little son Liu Dan and the state affairs to the prime minister Zhuge Liang. White King Town has so much to do with the Three Kingdoms that it is full of memorial spots. Each of the paintings on the ridges or eaves of the buildings tells a vivid story about the Three Kingdoms. In the ancient buildings of the town, many statues of the Three Kingdoms heroes are erected lifelike. Among them are Liu Bei, Zhuge Liang, Guan Yu and Zhang Fei in Mingliang Palace and Zhuge Liang and his father and son in the Temple of Marquis Wu.

White King Town is a museum of cultural relics. Assembled here are seventy-four pieces of stone engravings of the Sui, Yuan, Ming, Qing Dynasties, as well as countless poems, couplets, paintings and works of calligraphy left behind by the ancient people. Many famous poets of different dynasties, such as Li Bai, Du Fu, Bai Juyi, Liu Yuxi, Su Shi, Huang Tingjian, Fan Chengda, Lu You and others once toured and produced their celebrated works here. What's more, thousands of tools, weapons, instruments and other articles of different times are collected in the town. Among them are stone axes and stone arrows of the New Stone Age, bronze swords and axes of the slavery society, the serial bells of the Warring States, bronze mirrors of the Qin and Han Dynasties, celadon tiger cubs of the Shu Han, white porcelain painting box of the Tang Dynasty and gold-traced china bowls of the Song Dynasty... They will all be the guides to show you to the splendid culture of the Yangtze Gorges.

鳳凰碑，碑上刻有號稱鳥中之王的鳳凰、花中之王的牡丹、樹中之王的梧桐，故又稱三王碑。

Phoenix Stele Engraved on the stele are phoenixes, king of birds, peony, king of flowers and Chinese parasol, king of trees, so it is also called "Three Kings Stele".

竹葉詩碑，由一叢竹葉組成一首詩文，融詩、畫、金石於一碑，構思別致。

Bamboo Blades Poem Stele A bamboo blades pictographic poem is engraved on the stele, the art of stone carving, poetry and painting ingeniously integrated.

粉 壁 牆

"舉目眺白鹽，碑刻銘千古"。夔門南岸的鹽山上，有一塊斑白的巨石，高數十米，寬千餘米，壁立江畔，如同一堵粉白的牆壁，上面滿是摩崖題刻，行、楷、隸、篆、草書，應有盡有，風格各異，琳瑯滿目。

粉壁牆石刻，自宋迄今，展示了我國歷代的書法藝術。字體最大的是近人孫元良將軍的"夔門天下雄，艦機輕輕過"，每字有一人多高。字體最小而文字最多的是南宋書法家趙公碩書寫的《宋中興聖德頌》，全文980多個字，大的五尺見方，小的如指頭大小，刻在高約4米、寬約7米範圍內，是一方罕見的巨型壁刻。清人張伯翔所書"瞿塘"，劉心源所書"夔門"，蒼勁有力，古樸凝重，與巍峨夔門交相輝映。

THE WHITEWASHED WALL

"Looking up at Whitewashed Wall of Mt. Baiyan one sees
The engravings by different people in different times."

As the lines describe, there is a huge white rock on Mt. Baiyan at Kuimen on the southern side of the gorge. The rock is dozens of metres high and more than a thousand metres broad, facing the river like a whitewashed wall, and it is covered with engraved inscriptions in running hand, cursive hand, regular script, official script, or seal character. Almost all styles of all schools of calligraphy can be found on the rock.

Ever since the Song Dynasty, the rock engraving on the Whitewashed Wall has been revealing the essence of the art of Chinese calligraphy. The largest characters on the rock are those by Sun Yuanliang, a contemporary general. The words read *"Kuimen stands in splendour and sails pass in silence."* Each of the characters is taller than a man. And the characters by Zhao Gongshuo, a calligrapher of the Song Dynasty, are the smallest in size and largest in number. The whole text of 980 words of *Ode to the Resurgence of the Song* was engraved on the rock. The largest characters are five inches square and the smallest as tiny as a finger. The engraving covers a surface of about four metres high and seven metres broad. It is a rare huge rock engraving. Among the other engravings are "Qutang" by Zhang Boxiang and "Kuimen" by Liu Xingyuan, of the Qing Dynasty. The characters appear bold and vigorous setting off the landscape of Kuimen beautifully.

粉壁牆 The Whitewashed Wall.

翹首望夔峰，何須再登山？
Raise your head and see the Kui Peak.
Do you have to scale the mountain?

倒吊和尚
Monk Hung Upside-Down.

孫元良將軍的題刻："夔門天下雄，艦機輕輕過。"
" Kuimen stands in splendour and sails pass in silence",
engraved inscription by General Sun Yuanliang.

孟良梯
Meng Liang Ladder.

古 棧 道

蜀道難，難於上青天！古代三峽的交通，全靠水路，每遇洪水，祇好停航，旅行斷絕。直至清光緒年間，棧道聯通，三峽交通才得以改善。

三峽棧道分爲兩種，一種是在絕壁上開鑿的，途中有石橋連結溝壑的棧道，這種棧道貫穿三個峽段，高出江面數十米，寬二、三米，工程險要艱難，令人心悸目眩。《戰國策·秦策》有"棧道千里，通蜀漢"之說。瞿塘峽北岸絕壁邊十公里長的棧道，就是古代勞動人民身依絕壁，下臨大江，在刺破青天的岩壁上鑿出的一條石路，路寬五六尺，能過八人大轎，鑲嵌在千仞峭壁之腰，"驚濤駭浪建瓴下，顛崖撲谷相吐吞。"

另一種是沿着絕壁鑿孔打樁，墊板攀援而上的棧道。這種棧道主要分佈在瞿塘峽和小三峽內。如瞿塘峽中的孟良梯就是殘留下來的棧道石孔。石孔深和口徑各一尺，四四方方，孔與孔相距三尺，自下而上直到半山腰。相傳，宋朝名將楊繼業被奸臣害死後，屍骨埋在白鹽山頂的望鄉台上。楊繼業的親信孟良懷念他，想把他的屍體悄悄搬走，就在一天深夜，在峭壁上鑿石穿孔，架木爲梯，攀援而上，不料才至半山腰，被一個和尚發現，他佯裝雞叫，孟良以爲天亮，前功盡棄。後來，孟良發現是和尚作祟，盛怒之下就將和尚倒懸在山岩上，讓世人唾罵。

ANCIENT PLANK ROADS

"The road to Shu is harder than to cilmb to the sky."

In ancient times. all communications in the Yangtze Gorges region depended on the waterway. Whenever the flood came. the sails had to come to a halt and the travel in the region became impossible. Not until the years of Guangxu's reign in the Qing Dynasty was the plank road of the gorge region opened and the communications improved.

There are two kinds of plank roads — the one cut out of the cliffs with ravines spanned by flagstones. and the one protruded from the cliffs with the planks supported by piles driven into the cliffs. The former runs through the region of the Yangtze Gorges. The road is two or three metres wide and dozens of metres above the river. The project was both difficult and dangerous. Some sections of the road were cut by people of the remote past. Recorded in *Strategies of the Warring States — the Strategy of Qin* is "long miles of plank roads lead to the Shu Han (the present-day Sichuan Province)". The ten kilometres cut out of the precipice on the north side of Qutang Gorge is a wonder created by the working people of ancient times. The road of this section is five to six feet wide and a sedan-chair carried by eight people can pass it easily. From the road one can overlook thousands of valleys connected with one another and the roaring river flowing by.

The other kind of plank road. however. is built along the precipices by cutting holes in the rock and setting piles in the holes to support the planks. Such plank roads are mostly distributed in Qutang Gorge and the Lesser Three Gorges. Meng Liang Ladder, for instance. is the remains of this kind of plank road. It is made up of a flight of holes reaching halfway up the cliff. The holes are one foot cubic and three feet between each other. As the legend has it. in the Song Dynasty a noted general named Yang Jiye was murdered by treacherous officials and was buried at Wangxiangtai on the top of Mt. Baiyan. which was guarded by soldiers. Meng Liang. one of Yang's followers. cherished so much the memory of Yang that he tried to bring back the body. One day late at night he began to cut holes in the cliff trying to set a ladder to reach the grave. He was . however. overheard by a monk. who mimicked the crow of a cock for a prank. On hearing the crow. Meng Liang had to give up his task. thinking that dawn was breaking. So the task was only half done. Meng Liang flew into a rage when he knew it was the monk who had played a prank upon him. and he hanged the monk upside-down on the cliff so that people would curse and spit at him.

遊客爭看古棧道　Tourists eager to see the ancient plank road.

絕壁凌空古棧道
Ancient plank road high up the precipice.

棧道縴痕　Tracking rope marks.

架設航標燈，夜 晚 的 三峽江面上，一盞盞航標燈宛如顆顆明珠鑲在懸崖上，撒在激流中。目前，由重慶到吳淞口的航標，共設置了4000多座，其中以天險三峽的航標最爲重要。

Setting up beacons At night, beacon lights glimmer all along the Yangtze Gorges like bright pearls inlaid on the cliffs or scattered on the surging river. Of the more than 4,000 beacons along the line from Chongqing to Wusongkou, the ones in the Gorges are the most important.

棧道，全長約五、六十公里。 Plank roads in the gorge region, full length 50-60km.

風箱峽之謎

風箱峽，與孟良梯隔江相對，在一處黃褐色的懸岩絕壁上，有幾條豎立的岩穴裂縫，從中露出一些長方形的木匣，高約幾十米，可望不可及。有人說它是魯班幫大禹治水，疏通三峽時用過的風箱，故稱為風箱峽。也有人說它是諸葛亮藏兵書寶劍的兵書匣。古往今來，它像謎一樣令人猜想。

1971年，幾個身懷攀岩絕技的人，終於解開了這個千年之謎。原來，木匣是戰國時期巴人的岩棺，內有巴式銅劍、紡輪、木梳、草鞋、錢幣等一批十分珍貴的文物。

The Mystery of Fengxiang Crevices

Fengxiang Crevices, as it is named, consists of some vertical crevices on the brown-coloured precipice facing Meng Liang Ladder across the river. Some rectangular wooden boxes can be seen set in the crevices. The boxes are dozens of metres high within sight but beyond reach. Some said they were blacksmith's bellows left there by Lu Ban, a legendary craftsman, who came to help Yu, the legendary emperor of the Xia Dynasty, dredge the river. So the place was named Fengxiang, meaning bellows. Others said that the boxes were the containers for Zhuge Liang to hold his tactics books and swords. Throughout the ages the boxes remained mysterious.

It was not until 1971 when some skilled climbers got up to the crevices that the age-old enigma was solved. The boxes turned out to be the coffins of the Ba people of an ancient tribe in the period of the Warring States. Inside the coffins were such precious cultural relics as bronze Ba swords, loom wheels, wooden combs, straw shoes and coins.

風箱峽
Fengxiang crevices.

大溪文化遺址

位於瞿塘峽下口的大溪西岸，曾於一九五九年在此進行了兩次大規模的發掘工作，發現了一處距今約６千年至４千年的新石器時代原始人社會後期的村落遺址，出土了大量的陶器、石器、骨器、玉器等。大溪文化，屬長江流域的重要古文化。

The Remains of Daxi Culture

In 1959, two archaeological excavations were made in Daxi, at the east mouth of Qutang Gorge west of the river. Ruins of villages of the New Stone Age and the late stage of the slave society, about 4,000-6,000 years ago, were unearthed together with a great many pottery, stone, bone, and jade wares. Daxi Culture is an important ancient culture of the Yangtze valley.

錯開峽
Cuokai Gorge.

巫　峽

巫山十二峰
皆在碧虛中

　　"瞿塘迤邐盡，巫峽崢嶸起"。當你乘巨輪穿過一段山舒水緩的寬谷地帶，便進入了奇峰綿延、峭壁夾岸、美如畫廊的巫峽。巫峽因巫山得名，西起巫山城東的大寧河口，東至湖北省巴東縣的關渡口，全長45公里，整個峽谷奇峰削壁，羣巒疊嶂。船行其間，忽而大山當前，似乎江流受阻；忽而峰迴路轉，又是一水相通。咆哮的江流，不斷變換着方向，忽左忽右，七彎八繞，令人目不暇接。

　　幽深秀麗的巫峽，處處有景，景景相連，最爲壯觀的則是著名的巫山十二峰。這些山峰神態各異，有的若龍騰霄漢，有的似鳳凰展翅，有的青翠如屏，有的彩雲纏繞，有的常有飛鳥棲息於蒼松之間。而其中神女峰則最令人神往。還有與巫峽相連的大寧河、香溪、神農溪，青山綠水，風景別致，充滿山野情趣。

　　巫峽中有巫山、巴東、秭歸等峽中名城，名勝古跡多而悠久，風土人情妙趣橫生，令人流連忘返。

巫峽
Wu Gorge.

"While the magnificence of Qutang Gorge is left behind, the splendour of Wu Gorge comes in sight." Coming out of Qutang Gorge and sailing through an open area where the hills are low and the river is gentle, you enter Wu Gorge, which is characterised by beautiful peaks and steep cliffs on either side.

Wu Gorge is named after Mt. Wushan. It extends eastward from the mouth of the Daning River in the east of Wushan Town, Sichuan Province, to Guandukou in Badong County, Hubei Province, with a length of forty-five kilometres. The gorge is flanked with towering peaks and steep cliffs. Downstream you have to go through countless twists and turns. The river now seems to be blocked by the huge mountains, now breaks through and changes its direction. The changing course of the roaring river makes it difficult for you to take your bearings.

The deep gorge is so kaleidoscopic that you may feast your eyes on the beautiful scenes everywhere all along. The twelve peaks of Mt. Wushan make up a most spectacular scene. The peaks are varied in shape and posture. Some look like dragons flying to the sky, some like phoenixes spreading their wings and others like green screens. Some are shrouded in the cloud and others covered with ancient pinetrees. Among them Shennu (Fairy) Peak is most enchanting. The landscapes of the Daning River, Xiangxi River and Shennong river provide a unique flavour of primitiveness with the green mountains and the blue water.

In addition, located in the region of Wu Gorge are such famous walled cities as Wushan, Badong and Zigui, where there are a number of noted historical sites and where the folkways are so unique and colourful that one can enjoy himself heartily.

銀裝素裹　Pure and spangling snow.

峡江初春
Early spring in the gorge.

1 霞光伴船歸
Returning boats in sunset glow.

2 孔明碑
Zhuge Liang Niche—engraving allegedly
by Zhuge Liang.

3 楚蜀鴻溝
Wide chasm between Chu and Shu.

4 峭壁長廊
Long gallery of cliffs.

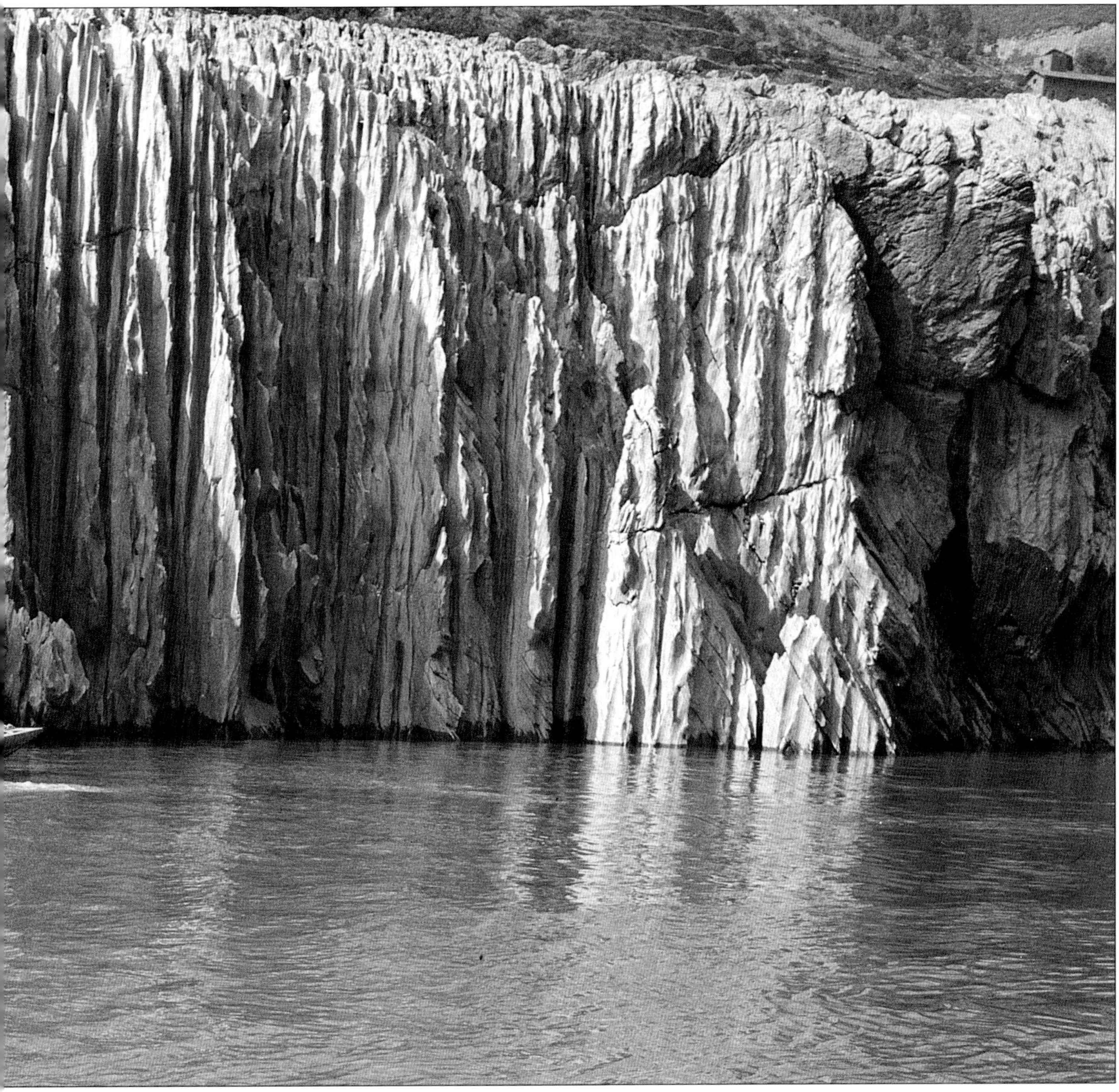

無奪橋　Wuduo Bridge.

峽險林更茂　Dangerous gorge and luxuriant trees.

輕舟過險灘
Skiff sailing down a dangerous shoal.

1 波光船影
Boats on glittering water.

2 金光一道破霧來
The sun radiating through mists.

3 曉嵐
Morning Haze.

風景勝地巫山

巫山是四川省最東部的一座古城，位於長江北岸大寧河與長江交滙處，山環水繞，風景迷人，名勝古跡甚多，素有"風景勝地"之稱。

巫山古城建有12條大街小巷，分別以巫山十二峰命名，充滿詩情畫意。尤其是起雲街，古建築與現代建築並存，古建築古色古香，現代建築挺拔雄偉，相映生輝，吸引着大批遊人。

巫山的風光名勝集中體現在三台八景十二峰。三台即：斬龍台、楚陽台、授書台。八景即：寧河晚渡、青溪魚釣、陽台暮雨、南陵春曉、夕霞晚照、澄潭秋月、秀峰禪利、女觀貞石。十二峰即：登龍、聖泉、朝雲、神女、松巒、集仙、聚鶴、翠屏、飛鳳、淨壇、起雲、上昇。這些名勝屹立巫峽兩岸，面臨滔滔大江，風光無限。

巫山物產豐富，土特產中以藥材、生漆和水果出名。大廟的黨參享有盛名，素稱廟黨。

WUSHAN, A FAMOUS SCENIC SPOT

Wushan is an ancient walled city in the eastern tip of Sichuan Province. Lying on the northern side of the gorge, where the Daning River and the Yangtze River converge, it is surrounded by mountains and rivers, famous for its scenic spots and historical sites.

The Wushan walled city consists of twelve streets named after the twelve peaks of Mt. Wushan and filled with poetic atmosphere. Qiyun Street, in particular, combines harmoniously the antiqueness of the ancient buildings with the magnificence of the modern ones, creating a great attraction to the tourists.

The landscape of Wushan is presented by "Three Terraces", "Eight Scenes" and "Twelve Peaks". The three terraces are "Dragon-Slaying Terrace", "Chu Terrace" and "Reading Terrace". The eight scenes are "Night of the Ninghe Ferry", "Angling by the Qingxi River", "Evening Rain at Yangtai", "Dawn in the Spring of Nanling", "Sunset Glow", "Autumn Moon Mirrored in the Clear Pool", "Temple Among Beautiful Peaks" and "the Taoist Temple and the Stones". The twelve peaks are Denglong (Soaring Dragon), Shengquan (Holy Spring), Chaovun (To-the-Cloud), Shennu (Fairy), Songluan (Pines), Jixian (Fairy-Gathering), Juhe (Flock-of-Cranes), Cuiping (Green Screen), Feifeng (Flying Phoenix), Jingtan (Purity Temple), Qiyun (Rising Cloud) and Shangsheng (Ascent). All these well-known scenic spots are located on either side of the gorge, facing the roaring river and offering ever-lasting charms.

Besides, Mt. Wushan is rich in natural resources. Among the most well known are medicinal herbs, raw lacquer and fruits. The *dangshen* produced in Damiao enjoys a world fame.

巫山峽口　Entrance of Wu Gorge.

巫山旅遊船碼頭
Wushan Cruise
Liner Harbour.

秀麗的巫峰
Serene and beautiful
eng Peak.

金盔銀甲峽

金盔銀甲峽雖是巫峽中的一段小峽，但風景名勝毫不遜色。這裏有橫石溪、老鼠洞、穿山箭、箭穿洞等奇特景觀。

橫石溪位於江北岸，平時溪水清澈見底，流水潺潺，暴雨時變成洪流飛瀑，奔騰而下，十分壯觀。

老鼠洞位於江南岸半山腰上，高、深約丈餘，洞口有一塊米黃色的岩石，遠遠望去，形如一隻老鼠，它前腿立起，後腿曲蹲，栩栩如生。

老鼠洞的東面有一石柱直指藍天，這就是穿山箭。傳說此箭是項羽留下的一支神箭，它射穿了北岸的一座山峰。

箭穿孔位於長江北岸朝雲峰下一座黑黝黝的山樑上。傳說當年楚霸王項羽與人比武，看誰能用箭射穿山樑。霸王拔弩張弓，祇用一箭就射穿了對面的山樑，留下了這個洞口。

JINKUIYINJIA GORGE

Jinkuiyinjia Gorge is a section of Wu Gorge. though short and small. the scenery of the area is as marvelous. The most fantastic is the Hengshi Brook. the Rat's Cave. the Mountain-Penetrating Arrow and the Arrow-Penetrated Hole.

The Hengxi Brook flows into the gorge from the north. The brook is usually clear and gentle but in the time of a heavy rain it becomes torrential offering a grand sight.

The Rat's Cave is situated halfway up in the cliff of the southern bank. about four metres deep. Just at the entrance of the cave stands a cream-coloured rock. From a distance the rock looks like a squatting rat with its four legs propping.

To the east of the Rat's Cave there is a column-shaped rock towering high into the sky. The rock is called Mountain-Penetrating Arrow. The legend has it that it was a magic arrow left there by Xiang Yu. a leader of the peasants' uprising army in the end of the Qin Dynasty. The arrow dropped there after piercing through a peak on the north side of the gorge.

The Arrow-Penetrated Hole is spotted on the black ridge of the mountain just at the foot of Chaoyun (To-the-Cloud) Peak. It is said that Xiang Yu once had a shooting contest with someone to see who could shoot through the ridge of the mountain with an arrow. Xiang Yu succeeded with the first arrow. The hole was thus left there.

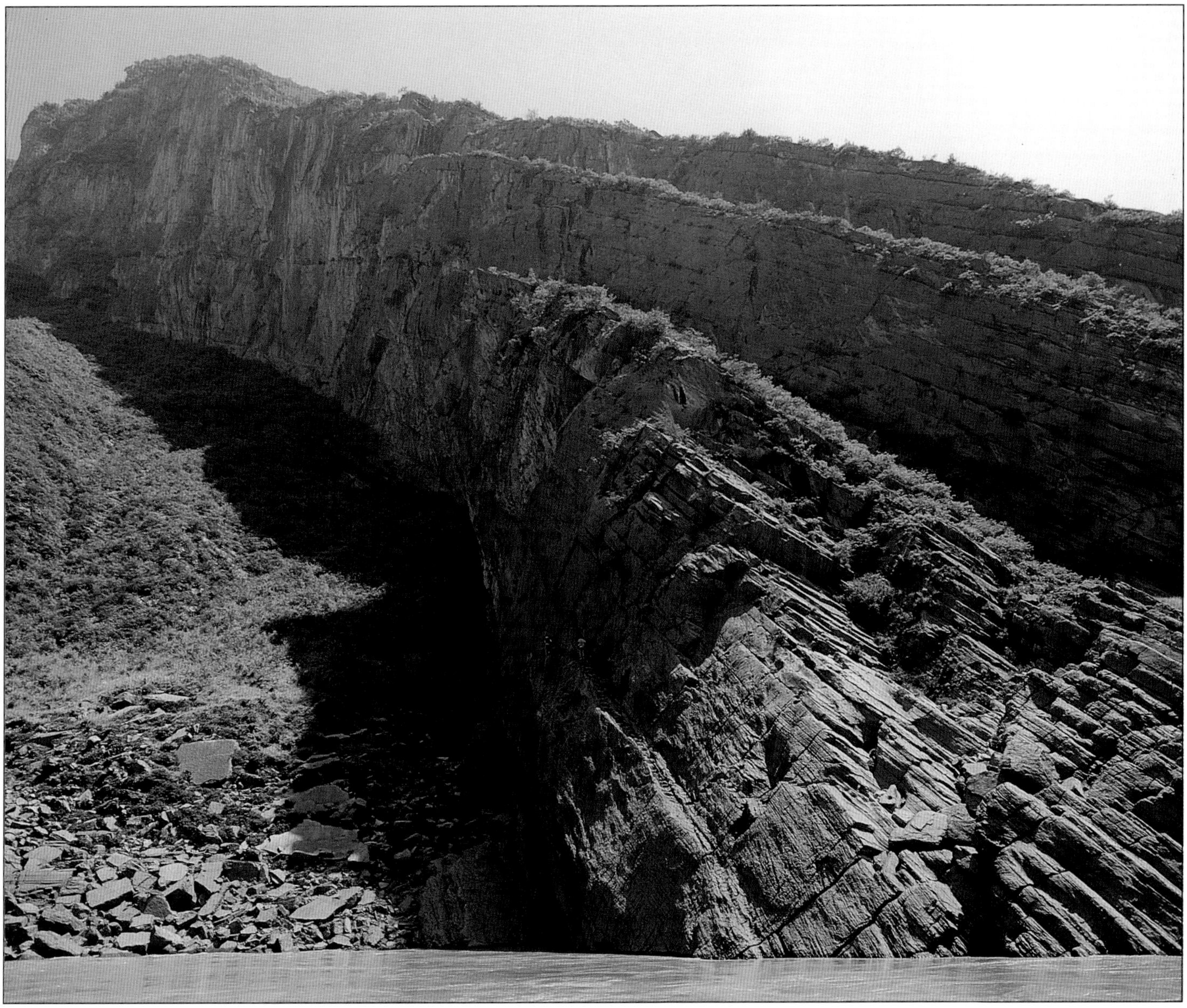

1 金盔銀甲峽
  Jinkuiyinjia Gorge.

2 龍脊石
  Dragon Back Rock.

3 箭穿洞
  Arrow-Penetrated Hole.

4 箭石
  Arrow Stone.

巫山十二峰

"放舟下巫峽，心在十二峰"。

巫山十二峰屹立長江兩岸，北岸六峰——登龍、聖泉、朝雲、神女、松巒、集仙。南岸三峰——聚鶴、翠屏、飛鳳。這九峰均在江邊，可一覽無餘。還有淨壇、起雲、上昇三峰，由於"隔山之表"，如欲遊覽，須從青石溪上行，方可領略其英姿。

爲了便於遊人記憶，古代文人將十二峰名聯成一首七言詩：

　　神女朝雲千古談，
　　聚鶴過江飛集仙。
　　翠屏青葱松巒綠，
　　飛鳳授書瑤姬傳。
　　登龍騰空六峰攢，
　　獅子銀牌飲聖泉。
　　起雲上昇何處去，
　　小溪河畔訪淨壇。

巫山十二峰，峰峰雲纏霧繞，幽深秀麗。而最多情、最秀麗的則是神女峰。

神女峰位於長江北岸，與青石鎮隔江相望。這個高約十米、環圍六米左右的人形石柱，屹立在海拔1020米的山巓上。每當晨曦初照或黃昏時，神女峰白雲繚繞，彩霞輝映，遠遠望去，就像一位亭亭玉立的少女，含情脈脈地凝視着江面。神女峰不僅峰姿秀麗，而且傳說動人。相傳，神女是西天王田的幼女瑤姬的化身。她邀十二仙女下凡，幫助大禹開鑿三峽，疏通九水。她還爲樵夫驅虎豹，爲農人保豐收，爲病人種靈芝，爲船民指點航向，深受百姓愛戴。千百年來，神女美麗動人的故事廣爲流傳。

THE TWELVE PEAKS OF MT WUSHAN

"Sailing downstream to Wu Gorge, I have my heart only in the twelve peaks of Mt. Wushan."

The twelve peaks of Mt. Wushan stand on both sides of the gorge. On the north there are six peaks — Denglong (Soaring Dragon), Shengquan (Holy Spring), Chaoyun (To-the-Cloud), Shennu (Fairy), Songluan (Pines), Jixian (Fairy-Gathering) — and on the south three — Juhe (Flock-of-Cranes), Cuiping (Green Screen) and Feifeng (Flying Phoenix). All the above nine peaks are so close to the river that you can take them in sight at a glance when sailing past. The sight of the other three peaks — Jingtan (Purity Temple), Qiyun (Rising Cloud) and Shangsheng (Ascent) — is blocked by the mountain. You can, anyhow, enjoy the view on shore walking upwards along the Qingshixi River.

In order to make it easy for tourists to remember the names of the twelve peaks, the names were composed into the following lines by some men of letters in the ancient times：

The Fairy is going up To-the-Cloud as the tale goes,
And a Flock-of-Cranes are flying to Fairy-Gathering peak.
The pines form a Green Screen for the fairy and the cranes,
To whom the Phoenix passes letters from Yao Ji in paradise.
The Soaring Dragon is now high over the six peaks watching
The lions drinking the Holy Spring and meanwhile wondering
Why does the Rising Cloud make such an Ascent and where to?
Oh, she's on a pilgrimage to Purity Temple by Xiaoxi River.

The twelve peaks which are often capped by mist and cloud appear both serene and elegant, and Shennu Peak stands most remarkable.

Shunnu Peak stands on the northern side of the gorge facing Qingshi Town across the river. The peak towers on the summit of the mountain 1,020 metres above sea level and the tip of the peak is a rock about ten metres in height and six metres in circumference. In the first rays of the morning sun or in the sunset glow, the white clouds float round the peak, creating a charming view. From a distance the peak looks like a slim and graceful young lady gazing at the river with great affection. Not only does Shennu Peak have a beautiful appearance but also have a moving tale related to it. As the tale goes, Shennu Peak as well as the other eleven peaks of the mountain are the fairies incarnate. Shennu is the incarnate of the little daughter of the queen of Heaven, named Yao Ji, who descended to the world with other fairies to help Yu, the emperor of the Xia Dynasty, to cut open the Yangtze Gorges and dredge the rivers. She drove away fierce beasts for woodmen, looked after crops for farmers, grew medicine herbs for the sick and set the course for boatmen, and she was thus loved by the local people. The moving tale about Shennu has been getting round for thousands of years.

從青石看巫山 Viewing Mt. Wushan from Qingshi.　　　　　**淨壇峰** Jingtan Peak.

神女峰　Shennu Peak.

集仙峰　Jixian Peak.

神女峰　Shennu Peak.

巫 山 雲 雨

"曾經滄海難爲水，除却巫山不是雲。"這是唐代詩人元稹對巫山雲彩的讚嘆。古往今來，無數人爲巫山雲雨所傾倒。獨特的峽谷氣候，使巫峽時而細雨濛濛，竟日難晴；時而雲纏霧繞，似若幻境；時而晨晴午雨，變化莫測；時而雨止天晴，白雲成帶。正如一首古詩所描繪的："巫山十二峰，皆在碧虛中。迴合雲藏日，霏微雨帶風"。巫山雲雨，令人叫絕！

巫山雲雨，因其綺麗多彩，虛幻莫測，給人以無限的情趣。那飄浮在十二峰上的白霧，似烟非烟，似雲非雲，似雨非雨，使巫山羣峰顯得絢麗多姿，恍如仙境；巫山的雨，來則濃雲滾滾，鋪天蓋地，像要覆蓋四野，淹沒大江，船行疑無路；雨止則縷縷淡雲在峽谷中悠悠飄蕩，忽聚忽散，變化萬千；雨後，則山川一碧如洗，峰青巒秀，彩霞萬朵。有時，還會出現東邊日出西邊雨，江南降雨江北晴，山上下雨山下晴的奇異景觀，令人大飽眼福。

THE RAIN AND CLOUDS OF MT WUSHAN

"Having been to a vast sea, one will never think much of the water in a river, and one will find no clouds appealing comparing them with those of the Wushan Mountain." That was how Yuan Zhen, a poet of the Tang Dynasty, marvelled at the clouds of Mt. Wushan, which, through the ages, have been admired by thousands of people, too. The unique climate of the gorge region produces varied scenes of different weathers in Wu Gorge. Mt. Wushan is sometimes shrouded in the fine drizzle all day long and sometimes twined by floating clouds and mists. Sometimes it rains in the morning and clears up in the afternoon, and sometimes the sunshine alternates with the rain, creating a sea of clouds after rain. In a word the change is unpredictable just as it is descibed in a poem:

On Wushan stand twelve peaks,
All in a visionary world one sees.
When the clouds hide the sun,
A rain will come with winds.

The rain and clouds of Mt. Wushan are so changeable and colourful that they are always appealing to the beholders. What is drifting around the peaks can not be exactly called cloud nor mist nor haze. It is something of the mixed feature that makes the peaks as fair as in a fairyland. The rain, on the other hand, usually comes with black clouds overcasting the mountains and the river, and the sails at the time seem to lose their courses. When the rain stops, the clusters of light clouds will linger in the valley, now converging and now dispersing, changing in various ways. After the rain the valley appears completely fresh, and rosy clouds set off green peaks and hills beautifully. Sometimes when the sun is shining in the east, it is raining in the west, or when it has cleared up in the north, the rain is still pouring in the south, or when it is drizzling on the top of the mountain, it is sunny at the foot. What wonderful views!

奇峰綿延，雲霧昇騰　Chains of peaks and seas of clouds.

峽谷幽深，雲雨繚繞
Deep serene valleys shrou
in clouds and mists.

峽口初晴
Misty gorge after rain.

峡雲雨
ouds and mists
Wu Gorge.

"五嶽歸來不看山，寧河歸來不看峽。"這是遊人對寧河小三峽的由衷讚美。大寧河發源於大巴山南麓，全長250公里，由北向南，在巫峽西口注入長江，是長江在三峽最大、最美的一條支流。小三峽位於大寧河下游，從巫山至大昌；由龍門峽、巴霧峽、滴翠峽組成，全長60公里。這裏"有山皆翠，有水皆綠，有峰皆奇，有瀑皆飛，"不是三峽，勝似三峽。

龍門峽古名雞門，因峽口有一巨石兀立，形似蘿卜，故素稱蘿門，峽長3公里，是小三峽中最短的一個峽。峽口兩岸峭壁高聳入雲，峰峰相對，宛若門戶，雄奇壯觀，其形勝宛如夔門，故又有夔門之稱。峽內有常年不涸、水花四濺的龍門泉；有高聳雲端、岩坎層叠的九龍柱；有浪濤洶湧的銀窩灘。

巴霧峽從東坪壩起至太平灘止，長10公里。峽內奇峰爭雄，怪石爭形，碧流爭湧。似人、似物、似獸的鐘乳石千姿百態："龍進虎出"、"馬歸山"、"猴子攬月"、"烏龜灘"……無不惟妙惟肖，並伴有許多美麗的傳說。

滴翠峽從雙龍的牛鼻洞至涂家壩，長20公里，是小三峽中最長最美麗多姿的一個峽。峽兩岸羣峰競秀，翠竹葱蘢。河面上，時而激流似箭，時而波平如鏡；在岩影波光中，常有成對鴛鴦戲水，羣猴攀枝。這裏有銀絲千縷的水簾洞；有栩栩如生的摩岩佛像；有終年烟雨濛濛、迷離恍惚的天泉飛雨；有高逾百丈、橫亘數里、金碧輝煌的"赤壁摩天"等風景名勝。

龍門峽　Longmen Gorge.

小三峡風光
Scenery of the Lesser
Three Gorges.

Back from the Five Mountains, ①
One wants not to tour other mountains.
Back from the Daning River,
One wants not to visit other gorges.

This is tourists' hearty praise of the Lesser Three Gorges along the Daning River. Daning is the biggest and loveliest tributary in the Yangtze Gorges region. It rises in the south foot of the Daba Mountain, flows 250km southward and joins the Yangtze at the west end of Wu Gorge. The Lesser Three Gorges, in turn, lie on the lower Daning, stretching from Mt. Wushan to Dachang for 60km. They are named Longmen, Bawu and Dicui. There is a saying about these gorges that "no mountain is not verdant; no water is not green; no peak is not peculiar, no fall is not swift". They are different from the Yangtze Gorges, and better.

The Longmen Gorge was named Luomen in ancient times. It is now often referred to as the "Radish Door", because at the entrance of the gorge there is a huge radish-shaped rock. This 3km -long gorge is the shortest of the three. At the entrance, precipitous cliffs tower into clouds and face each other closely across the river, thus forming a natural gate magnificent and spectacular. As it resembles Kuimen, the gorge entrance is also known as the "Small Kuimen". In the gorge, there are the never-drying, ever-splashing Dragon Door Spring, the sky-scraping, thousand-stepped Nine Dragon Pillar, and the torrent-washed Yinwo Shoal.

The 10km-long Bawu Gorge starts at Dongpingba and ends at the Taiping Shoal. Along the gorge, all fantastic peaks contend to gain supremacy, all grotesque rocks strive to show peculiarity, and all green waters race to surge forward. The stalactic structures of all descriptions resemble human beings, concrete things and animals, such as "Dragon In and Tiger Out", "Horse-Returning to Mountain", "Monkeys Reaching for the Moon", "Tortoise Shoal", etc. All are remarkably lifelike, and many have beautiful legends about them.

Dicui Gorge extends for 20km from the Bull Nose Cave at Shuanglong to Tujiaba. It is the longest and the most picturesque of the Lesser Three Gorges. On the banks, each peak seems more beautiful than the other, and the bamboo groves are luxuriantly verdant. The river dashes on like an arrow at one moment, and smooths down like a mirror the next. Mandarin ducks sail in pairs across the crags reflected in the river, and monkeys leap from branch to branch in the reflected sunlight. Other scenic spots include the Water Curtain Cave with thousands of silver threads hanging down, the lifelike rock statue of Buddha, the Dancing Rain from Heavenly Spring, drizzly and dreamy all the year round, as well as the 1000-foot-high splendid, magnificent "Sky-Scraping Red Wall", which stretches for a few miles.

---

① Five Mountains: Mt. Taishan in Shandong, Mt. Hengshan in Hunan, Mt. Huashan in Shaanxi, Mt. Hengshan in Shanxi and Mt. Songshan in Henan.

銀窩灘上飛舟激浪　Shooting the rapids down Yinwo Shoal.

懸棺
Coffins in precipice crevices.

馬歸山
Horse-Returning Mountain.

绵羊崖

1 滴翠峡
Dicui Gorge.

2 摩崖佛像
Stalactic Buddhas on cliff.

3 綿羊崖
Mianyang (sheep) Cliff.

4 馬渡河
Madu River.

5 仿古棧道
Imitation plank road.

6 青翠欲滴
Green and fresh all over.

翠谷輕舟 Skiff passing green valley.

跨河索橋 Chain bridge across the river.

白龍過江 . White dragon crossing the river.

巴 東 風 光

　　巴東位於長江南岸，地處巫峽與西陵峽之間，南依巴山，北臨大江，是川鄂兩省交通要衝和鄂西山區的門戶，有"鎖鑰港"之稱。

　　巴東歷史悠久，風光名勝眾多，有"巴山夜雨"、"烟寺曉鐘"、"鳳山夕照"、"鹿洞晴雲"、"古亭秋月"、"仙洞靈泉"、"壤溪晚渡"、"千米石屏"等八大景觀。其中，以"壤溪晚渡"和"千米石屏"最讓人流連。

　　"壤溪晚渡"又名神農溪晚渡。神農溪發源於神農架南坡，沿途接納17條溪澗，由北向南穿行於深山峽谷之中，至西壤口注入長江，全長60公里。神農溪有龍昌、鸚鵡、棉竹三峽，有"鄂西小三峽"之稱。龍昌峽裏，寶塔峰拔地而起，古戰場依稀可辨，兩岸絕壁，曲折迂迴，深若幽巷重門，雄偉壯觀，以"雄"見長。鸚鵡峽山巒聳立，灌木繁茂，碧流清泉，山花遍野，燕飛鳥鳴，以"秀"見長。棉竹峽兩岸山勢險峻，峭壁崢嶸，河體狹長，溪水洶湧，以"險"見長。

　　當你乘坐古式木船從棉竹峽漂流至龍昌峽時，你不僅會目睹巴船似箭離弦，溪水清澈見底，深潭碧綠可愛，泉眼飛瀑遍佈，以及巴人岩棺、原始扁舟、古老村落、土家風情，還會從中領略到大三峽所沒有的古樸、自然的野趣。

　　"千米石屏"又名格子河石林，位於巴東西南棗子坪鄉。這裏奇峰異石，千姿百態，青松挺拔，綠草如茵。30多座孤峰和7個洞穴，被三處草坪、四個一綫天、五座重門、六條巷道、八條幽巷相隔相通，縱橫交錯、宛如迷宮，與週圍穿心岩、九龍觀等景區相連，形成了方圓十多公里的格子河石林風景區。加之人們給奇石所取的那些饒有趣味的名字：天字碑、一綫天、蜂窩座、夫妻峰、雙峰駱駝、穿雲含石、觀音坐蓮台、豬八戒守門等，更爲石林增添了許多情趣。

淺灘行舟　Sailing down the shoal.

BADONG SCENES

Badong, situated on the south bank of the Yangtze between Wu Gorge and Xiling Gorge, with Mt. Bashan on the south and the Yangtze on the north, is known as the "key port" for its significant location on the communications hub between Sichuan and Hubei Provinces as well as the gateway to the western Hubei mountain areas.

With its long history, Badong boasts numerous scenic beauties to tourists. The eight main spots are "Night Rain of Mt. Bashan", "Dawn Bell of the Smoke Temple", "Sunset on Mt. Fengshan", "Cloudscape of the Deer Cave", "Autumn Moon Over the Ancient Pavilion", "Celestial Spring in the Immortals Cavern", "Dusk Ferry on the Rangxi Stream", and "Thousand-Meter Stone Screen", among which the last two are the top attractions.

Dusk Ferry on the Rangxi Stream is also known as Dusk Ferry on the Shennong River. Extending 60km from the south slope of Mt. Shennongjia to the Yangtze at Xirangkou, the Shennong River takes in 17 streams as it runs southward in the remote mountains and deep canyons. The river cuts its way through Longchang, Yingwu, and Mianzhu, known as the "Lesser Three Gorges of Western Hubei". Longchang Gorge is flanked by precipitous cliffs, where the Pagoda Peak towers over a dimly identifiable ancient battlefield. The twists and bends of the river reminds one of going into a house through endless doors or walking in a deep lane that keeps turning mystically. The magnificent and spectacular Longchang Gorge, therefore, is noted for its "grandeur"; Yingwu Gorge, among undulating mountains, where streams babble through lush bushes and birds chirp high and low across the flowering fields, is noted for its "beauty"; while Mian-

zhu Gorge, with mountains soaring behind the stern cliffs and boisterous torrents surging through the narrow passage, is noted for its "danger".

Drifting downstream in an ancient-style boat from Mianzhu Gorge to Longchang Gorge one will see local boats shooting by like arrows, limpid water showing the riverbed, and dark green pools, gurgling springs, tumbling waterfalls, ancient coffins lodged in cliff crevices, primitive skiffs, age-old villages, the Tujia nationality customs, etc., thus enjoying the natural simplicity of the wilderness that the Yangtze Gorges are devoid of.

The Thousand-Meter Stone Screen, also known as Gezi River Stone Forest, lies in Nanzaoziping Town in the southwest of Badong. It is a spot where each of the many fantastic peaks and grotesque rocks presents its unique shape, and tall, straight pine trees rise sheer out of verdant carpets of lush grass. More than thirty single peaks and seven caves are linked up by three meadows, four spots of "thread of sky" (extremely narrow passage between huge rocks, where only a streak of the sky is seen), five gates, six tunnels and eight deep lanes, all crisscross to make a labyrinth of the whole place, which, together with the nearby Chuanxin Rock, Nine Dragons Scene, etc., has formed the famous scenic spot of Gezi River Stone Forest, covering a circumference of over 10km. Besides, the stone forest area gets more charm and appeal from the names people have given to the grotesque rocks, such as Tianzi Tablet (tablet shaped like the Chinese character 天, pronounced as "tian"), Thread of Sky, Honeycomb Rock, Man-and-Wife Peak, Two-Humped Camel, Through Clouds with Stones, Goddess Guanyin on Lotus Throne, Pigsy Keeping Door, etc.

春到巴東 Spring coming to Badong.

灘多水急，駕舟漂流 Drifting down shoals and rapids.

碧綠清透的神農溪 The green Shennongxi River, clear as crystal.

鐘乳——象鼻 Stalactite—elephant's trunk.

齊心協力 United as one.

農溪
Shennongxi River.

格子河夫妻峰
Man-and-Wife Peak by Gezihe River.

一綫天
A thread of sky.

三 峽 奇 石

三峽的石，如三峽的風光一樣瑰麗多姿，風采迷人。它們有的雄偉挺拔，嶙峋崢嶸；有的小巧玲瓏，如花似玉。特別是在大寧河和神農溪的河灘上，那些大大小小的鵝卵石，色彩斑斕，令人愛不釋手。鵝卵石上，有不同的花紋，有的黑底白點，如雪花飛舞；有的紅白相映，若白雲襯着彩霞；有的珠圓玉潤，似潔白的珍珠。更吸引人的是那些象形石，如充滿詩情畫意的"南國之夏"、"巴山夜雨"；惟妙惟肖的"姜太公釣魚"、"女媧補天"，以及形形色色的"動物石"、"植物石"等，令人讚嘆，爭相收藏。

GROTESQUE STONES OF
THE YANGTZE GORGES

The stones on the banks are as magnificent, charming, and varied as the riverscape there. They range from lofty, steep and forbidding crags to dainty, graceful and exquisite boulders. And variegated are the alluring cobbles of various sizes on the banks of the Daning River and the Shennongxi River. These cobbles display all kinds of coloured patterns: some with white spots against a black background, a picture of snowflakes dancing at night; some with mixed red and white patches, like the rosy dawn setting off white clouds; others either round and white as pearls or glossy as jade. But the top attractions are the multi-shaped cobbles, such as the idyllic and picturesque "Summer in the South", "Night Rain of Mt. Bashan", the lifelike "Jiang Taigong Angling", "Nuwa Mending the Sky", as well as a great variety of "animal cobbles" and "plant cobbles" — all of these marvels of nature are tourists' favourite souvenirs.

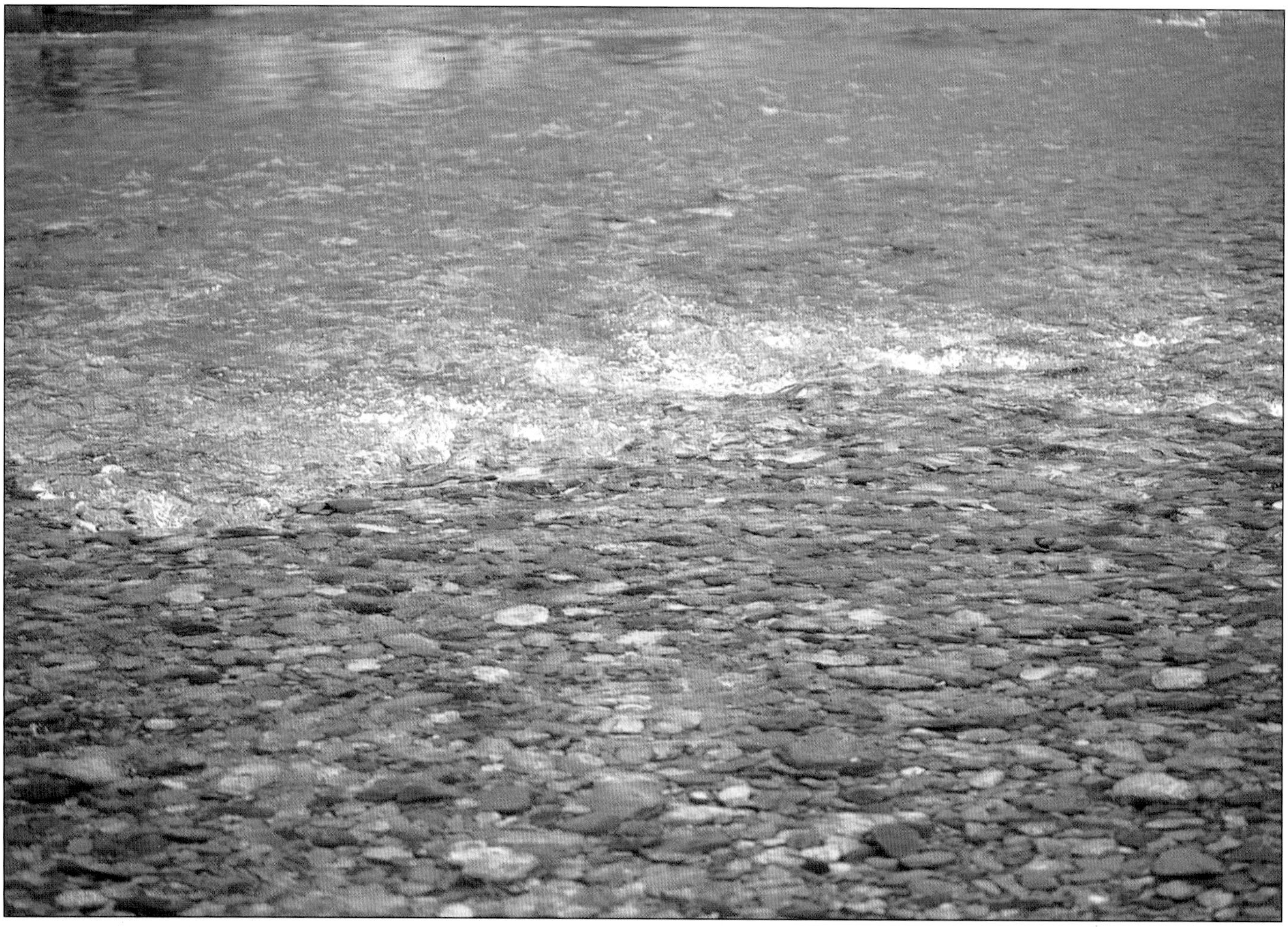

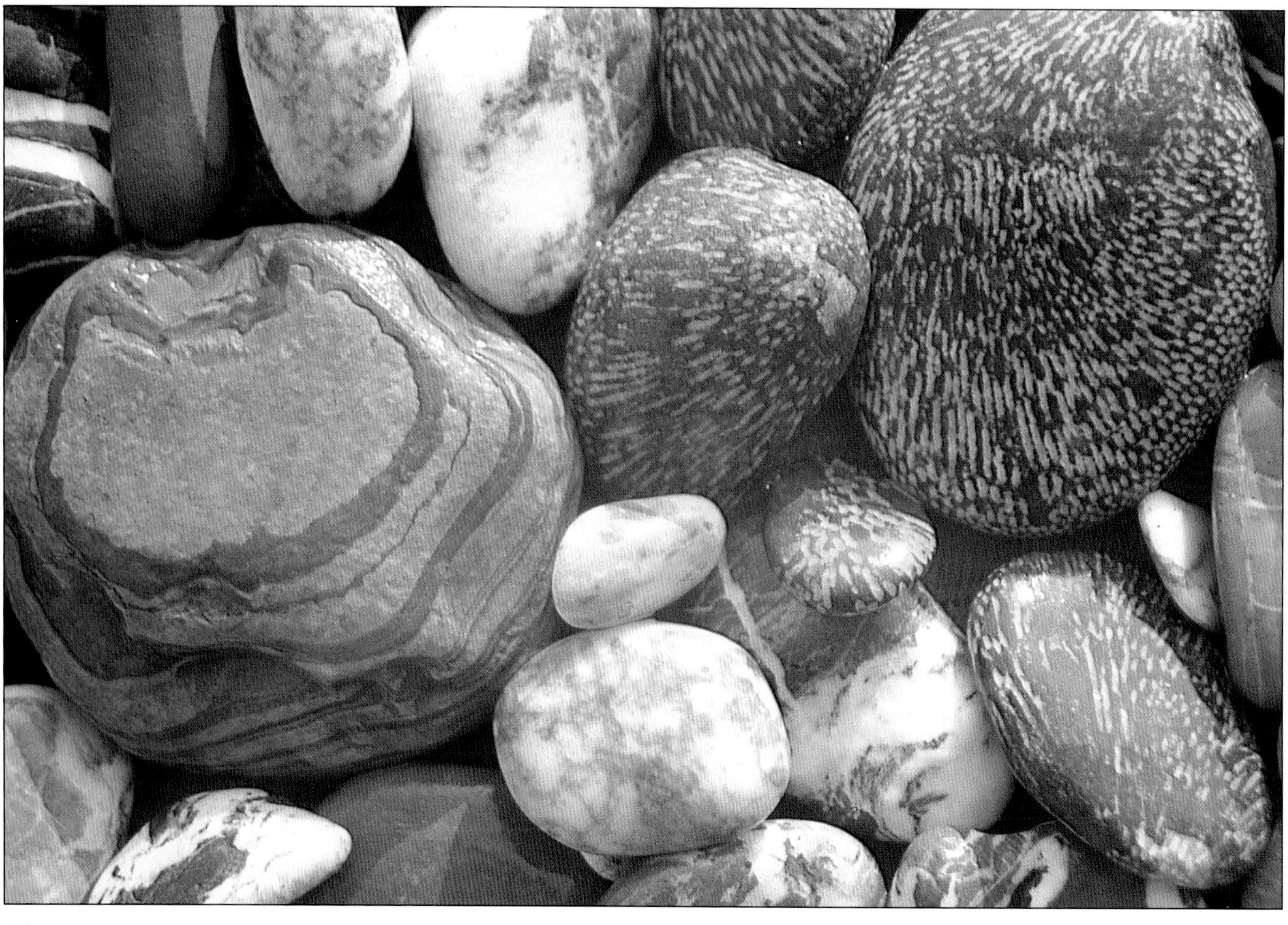

三峡石

"南國之夏"
'' Summer in the South''.

"踏花歸來"
'' Returning from Spring Outing''.

"姜太公釣魚"
'' Jiangtaigong Angling''.

"春江水暖鴨先知"
'' Duck Reporting the Coming of Spring''.

三峡石　Rocks of Yangtze Gorges.

十丈懸流萬堆雪
驚天如看廣陵濤

　"十丈懸流萬堆雪" 的西陵峽，西起秭歸縣的香溪河口，東至宜昌市的南津關，全長76公里。這裏峽中有峽，大峽套小峽；灘中有灘，大灘含小灘，灘多流急，以險著稱。

　"西陵灘如竹節稠，灘灘都是鬼見愁。" 昔日西陵有三大險灘，青灘、泄灘、崆嶺灘。灘險處，漩渦翻滾，水流如沸，驚險萬狀。由於航道狹窄，怪石橫陳，水亂流急，祇有空船才能過去。一首民謠中唱道："脚踏石頭手扒沙，當牛做馬把船拉，一步一鞭一把淚，恨得要把天地砸。" 解放後，航道上的險灘經過整治，如今航船已日夜暢通無阻了。

　峽內從西向東依次有兵書寶劍峽、牛肝馬肺峽、燈影峽、黃牛峽等。燈影峽一帶，不僅有掩映的飛瀑，還有奇特的石灰岩洞，神奇的傳說故事，為西陵峽增添了奇妙的色彩。

XILING GORGE

Xiling Gorge, described by an ancient poet as *"torrents from above falling upon ten thousand snow drifts"*, stretches 76km from the mouth of the Xiangxi River in Zigui County in the west to Nanjinguan Pass out of Yichang City in the east. All along Xiling there are gorges upon gorges and shoals upon shoals—small gorges hidden in bigger ones and small shoals set on bigger ones. With the great number of shoals and the swift torrents Xiling is well-known for its danger.

Like a bamboo full of joints is Xiling with its shoals,
And each one baffles even supernatural beings.

Xiling used to be more hazardous with the three most dangerous shoals: Qingtan Shoal, Xietan Shoal, and Kongling Shoal. Some places were extremely hazardous with turbulent whirls and boiling rapids. And in places where the channel got too narrow and where the boisterous torrent raced on like ponies among grotesque reefs, only empty boats were able to pass. An old folk rhyme goes:

Trampling upon rocks and clutching at sands,
Like oxen and horses we are hauling boats,
In tears we're whipped to crawl step by step,
And how we wish we could smash the evil world.

After liberation, however, the dangerous rocks and shoals were blasted away, and day-and-night navigation has since been made possible.

In Xiling Gorge lie a few small gorges from west to east in the following order: Tactics Books and Sword, Bull's Liver and Horse's Lung, Shadow Play, and the Ox Gorge. Along the Shadow Play Gorge, there are half-hidden waterfalls, peculiar karst caves and mystic legends, all adding greatly to the wonder of Xiling.

西陵烟雲　Mists and clouds in Xiling Gorge.

西陵峽　Xiling Gorge.

屈原故里秭歸城

　　秭歸位於長江北岸的臥牛山麓，因城垣形如"葫蘆"，故有"葫蘆城"之稱。又因城牆均由石頭疊砌而成，又叫"石頭城"。

　　秭歸是我國偉大的愛國詩人屈原的故里，他誕生在山青水秀的樂平里。屈原是一位具有遠見卓識的政治家，是中國文學史上第一位大詩人，是三峽裏的"第一流才子"。他憂國憂民，最後投汨羅江，以身殉國。屈原留下的《離騷》、《九章》、《九歌》等光輝詩篇，聲貫古今，名揚中外。

　　在樂平里，有關屈原的名勝古跡和傳說甚多，古人曾集為"八景"並以景名聯詩一首："降龍伏虎嘯天來，響鼓岩連擂鼓台。照面井寒奸佞膽，讀書洞出離騷才。坵生玉米合情操，濂滴珍珠蕩俗埃。鎖水回龍含澤畔，三閭八景勝蓬萊"。

　　秭歸還是歷史悠久的柑桔之鄉，屈原在他的名篇《桔頌》中，曾對桔樹的形象和性格作過深刻的描寫。今天，秭歸已成為我國七大柑桔生產基地之一。深秋時節，滿目都是柑桔林，青枝綠葉藏紅果，如詩如畫。

ZIGUI CITY, QU YUAN'S NATIVE PLACE

Zigui is located at the foot of Mt. Woniu on the north bank of the Yangtze. As the city wall is shaped like a gourd, it is also known as the "Gourd City", and, stone walled, it is sometimes called the "Stone City".

Zigui is the native place of Qu Yuan, the great poet and patriot born over 2,000 years ago to the green hills and clear waters of Lepingli. Besides being a statesman with foresight and sagacity, Qu Yuan has been established as the earliest great poet in the Chinese literature and is referred to as the "No. 1 Talent of the Yangtze Gorges". He was so deeply concerned over the fate of his nation that he ended up drowning himself in the Miluo River in despair when he failed to help save his kingdom, leaving behind brilliant poems such as *Li Sao*, *Jiu Zhang*, *Jiu Ge*, etc., which are famous throughout the times and all over the world.

Lepingli abounds with legends and sites concerning Qu Yuan. Among the eight major scenic spots are the Mirror Well, the Study Cave, the Pearl Curtain, etc.

Zigui also has a long history as a land of oranges. *Ode to Tangerine*, one of Qu Yuan's best poems, renders a detailed description of the shape and character of orange trees. Zigui has now developed into one of China's seven orange bases. The place is especially idyllic and picturesque in late autumn, when the orange and tangerine trees all over the hills become overloaded with golden fruits half-hidden among the green foliage.

屈原祠 Qu Yuan Temple.

秭歸縣遠眺 A long shot of Zigui County.

綠水悠悠話香溪

香溪鎮位於長江北岸香溪河與長江交滙處，鎮的東面，香溪清澈碧綠，像一條玉帶從遠方緩緩飄來，滙入長江。香溪河畔的寶坪村是漢代明妃王昭君的故鄉。「昭君自有千秋在，胡漢和親見識高。」「昭君出塞」的故事，流傳千古，家喻戶曉。人們把她看成是三峽裏的「第一流佳人」。

乘船至香溪昭君台後，西行6公里，越過香溪河橋，便可到風景秀美的寶坪村（明妃村）一遊。寶坪村有許多處紀念王昭君的名勝古跡，如昭君祠、昭君院、楠木井、梳妝台、繡鞋洞等，以及許許多多有關昭君的美麗故事和傳說。

"NO. 1 BEAUTY" ON THE GREEN XIANGXI RIVER

The town of Xiangxi sits on the north bank at the confluence of the Xiangxi River and the Yangtze. On the east of the town, the limpid, green Xiangxi River, like a jade belt, flows lazily from afar into the Yangtze. Baoping, a village on the Xiangxi River, is the birthplace of Wang Zhaojun, the celebrated imperial concubine of the Han Dynasty. The story of Wang Zhaojun married into a northern kingdom, handed down from ancient times, is known to every household in China. She is regarded as the "NO. 1 Beauty" of the Yangtze Gorges.

Take a boat to Zhaojun Terrace on the Xiangxi River, head westward for 6km, and cross the Xiangxi River Bridge, then you can go sightseeing in the picturesque Baoping Village (or Imperial Concubine Village), where you will see Zhaojun Temple, Zhaojun Courtyard, Nanmu Well, the Dressing Table, the Embroidered-Shoe Cave and various other Zhaojun memorial sites. You will also hear many beautiful stories and legends about Wang Zhaojun.

飛來廟　Feilai Temple.

香溪雲霧 Xiangxi River in mists.

相傳昭君汲水的楠木井
Nanmu Well, where Zhaojun is said to
have fetched water.

昭君村的昭君宅
Zhaojun's former residence in Zhaojun Village.

似人若物三名峽

西陵峽中的兵書寶劍峽、牛肝馬肺峽和燈影峽，似人若物，最富情趣。

"兵書寶劍"位於長江北岸，峭壁上有一叠層次分明的岩石，形似書卷堆放，人稱"兵書"。在兵書的側面，有一塊石頭，形如寶劍，插入江中，即所謂"寶劍"。相傳諸葛亮晚年時，將平生用兵之計寫成一部兵書，因蜀中無人可授，又恐落入亂臣手中，故將兵書寶劍藏於大峽之中，讓後世勇士取拿。天長日久，兵書和寶劍就化作了岩石。

牛肝馬肺峽位於長江北岸青灘下十餘里處。在半山腰石壁間，東邊懸掛一團赭黃色的頁岩，形似牛肝；兩邊垂下一堵黯褐色的岩石，酷象馬肺，形態逼真，故人稱之牛肝馬肺峽。歷經滄桑，怪石依然如故，爲人們爭睹。

燈影峽位於西陵峽的東段，緊靠石牌鎮。山上有四塊奇石兀立，狀如《西遊記》中唐僧師徒四人的模樣。四塊奇石在落日餘輝的映照下，更是活靈活現：孫猴子手搭凉棚，豬八戒挺着圓肚，沙和尚昂首闊步，唐三藏指手於後，映於天幕之上，酷似燈影戲中的角色，故人稱燈影峽。

GORGES FAMOUS
FOR LIFELIKE ROCKS

The rocks known as Tactics Books and Sword. Bull's Liver and Horse's Lung. and Shadow Play are true to life. hence a good fun.

Tactics Books and Sword on the top of a north bank cliff is a stack of rock slabs that resemble a pile of books. called "tactics books". and a sword-shaped rock on one side. which is thrust in the river. referred to as "sword". The legend goes that Zhuge Liang. in his remaining years. wrote books of tactics he had used in all of his military life. As there was no one in Shu (his native place. a kingdom then) so gifted as to be able to learn his tactics and as Zhuge wanted to keep the books out of the reach of the treacherous court officials. he ended up hiding the books and his sword in the gorge for valiant people of later ages to find. The books and the sword. however. have turned into stone with the passage of time.

Bull's Liver and Horse's Lung are rocks about 10 *li* down Qingtan Shoal on the north bank. From a cliff halfway up the mountain suspended a lump of reddish brown shale in the east. which is shaped like a bull's liver. and a dark brown rock in the west resembling a horse's lung. Both are strikingly true to life. hence the name "Bull's Liver and Horse's Lung". Thousands upon thousands of years have passed. these rocks are still there. jutting out in their old peculiar way. unravished. for tourists to marvel at.

Close to Shipai Town at Mt. Shibi on the south bank is the Shadow Play. where four grotesque rocks rise in the shapes of four legendary figures in *Journey to the West*. These rocks are most lifelike in the setting sun—Monkey Sun making an awning with his palm. Pigsy sticking out his pot-belly. Monk Shaseng striding vigorously ahead and Monk Xuanzang pointing forward in the rear—all silhouetted against the sky in the twilight so much similar to the figures in the shadow play that people named the rocks "Shadow Play".

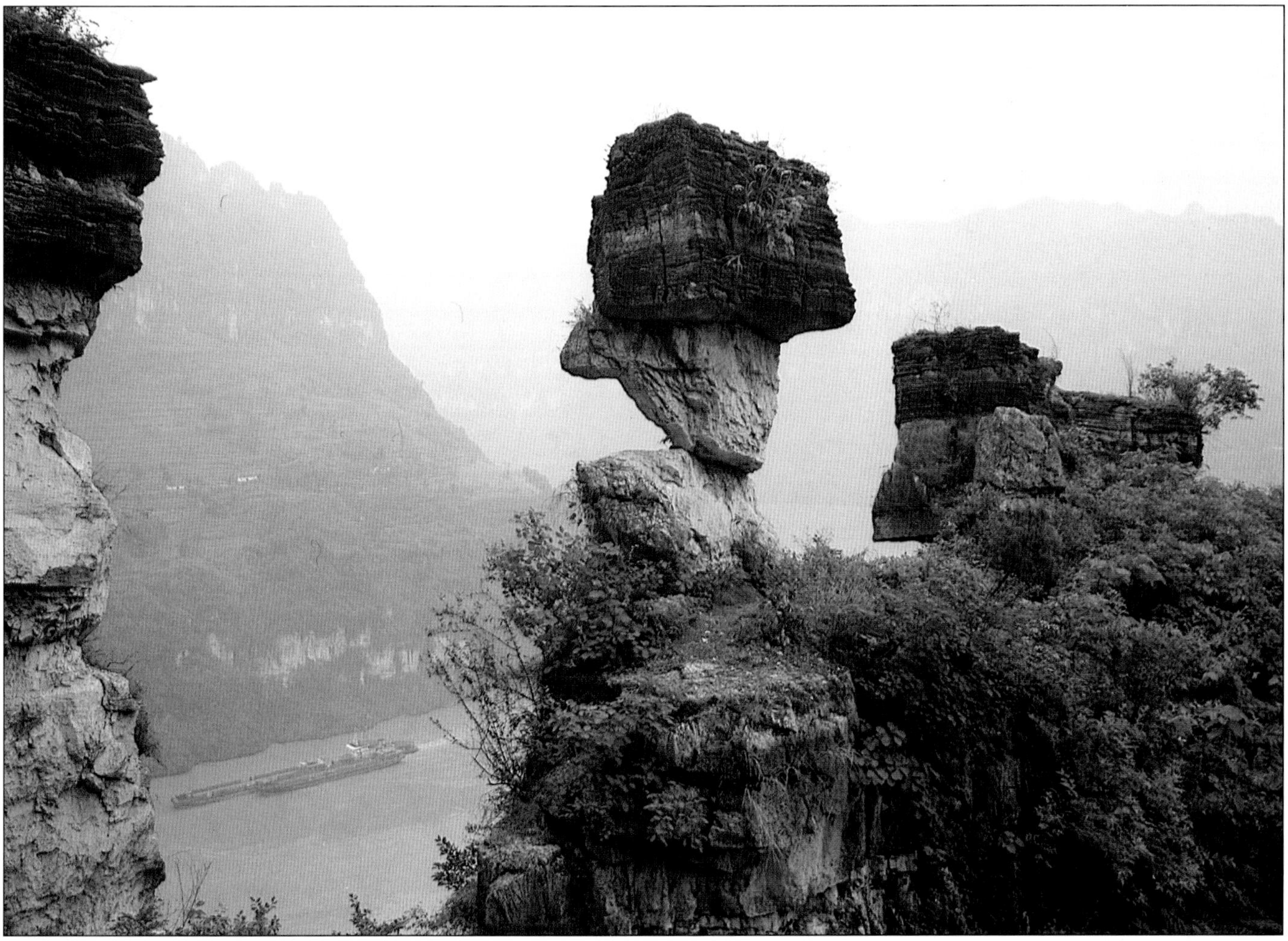

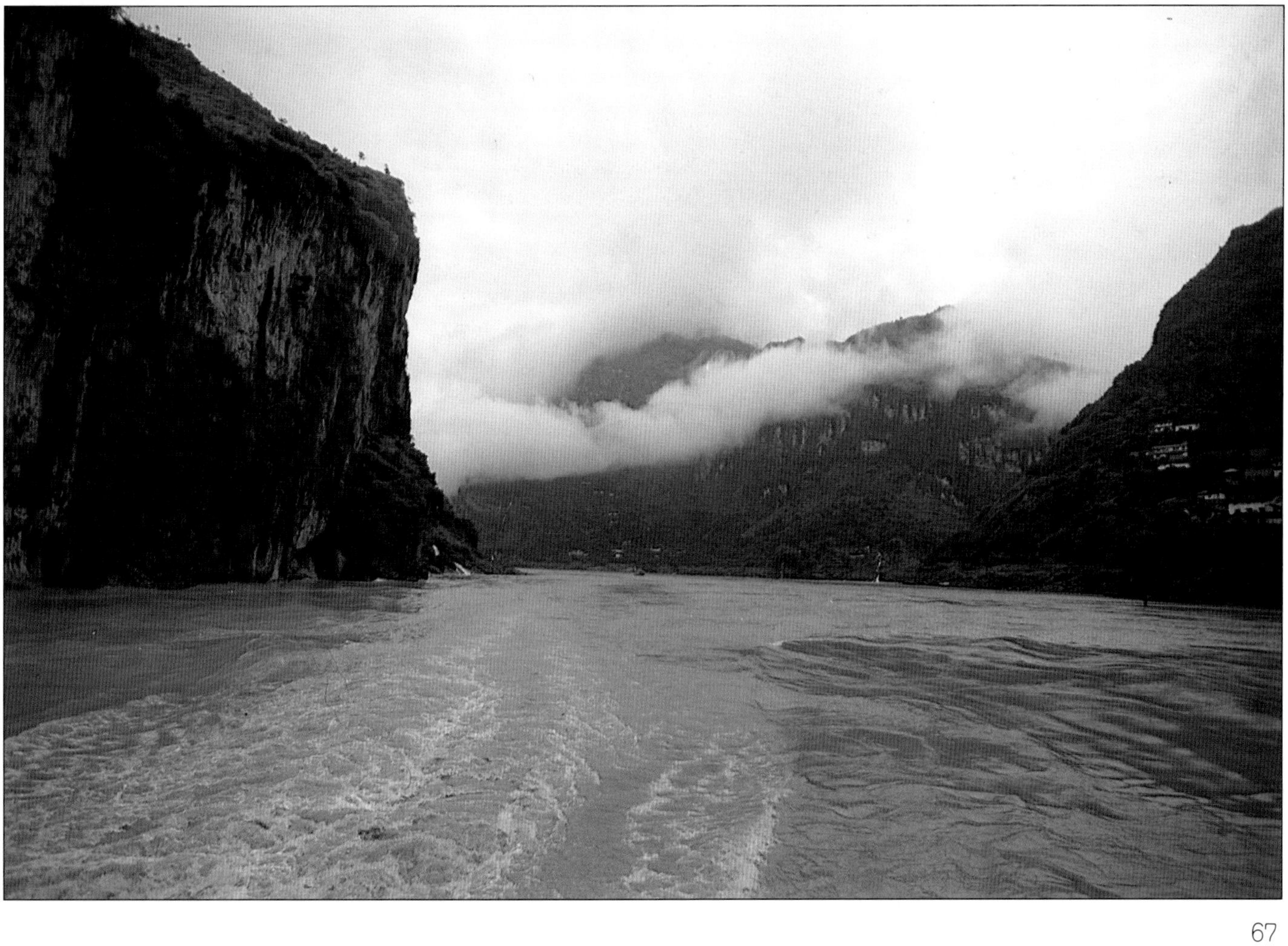

峽 中 名 灘

三峽險灘中，以青灘和崆嶺灘最爲有名。

青灘位於兵書寶劍峽與牛肝馬肺峽之間。灘長1.5公里，從西至東依次分爲頭灘、二灘、三灘，灘中亂石如林，白浪翻滾，水流甚急，人稱入江“鐵門坎”。來往船隻下灘急如箭，上灘如登梯，祇有走“Ｓ”形航道才能通過，古人曾用“扁舟轉山曲，未舟已先驚”來形容此處的險情。

崆嶺灘位於廟河段大江中，向有“青灘洩灘不算灘，崆嶺才是鬼門關”之說。灘內礁石林立，犬牙交錯。由大珠、頭珠、二珠、三珠等24處礁石組成。其中大珠像一條大鯊魚縱臥江心，把江流分爲南北兩漕，南漕亂石密佈，泡漩無常；北漕彎曲狹窄，暗礁如林。灘中原有一個“對我來”礁石，令人望而生畏。凡船隻經此過灘，祇能左避右讓，穿縫航行。

解放後，經過多次炸礁疏浚，已化險爲夷。特別是葛洲壩工程興建後，水位昇高，昔日的險灘已變爲坦途。

PROMINENT SHOALS IN THE YANGTZE GORGES

Of all the most dangerous shoals in the Gorges, Qingtan and Kongling are the best known.

Stretched between "Tactics Books and Sword" and "Bull's Liver and Horse's Lung", Qingtan — First Shoal, Second Shoal, and Third Shoal—runs 1.5km from west to east, teeming with reefs and convulsed with sweeping, boisterous rapids, an "Iron Threshold" to the river. Boats and skiffs used to shoot downstream like flying arrows and flounder upstream as if scaling a ladder, zigzagging their way either up or down. One ancient poet described these breathtaking journeys as follows:

So dangerous rapids the boat is to shoot.

And so fast your heart beats before you start.

Kongling Shoal lies in the Temple Reach of the river. The local people have always said, "Qingtan and Xietan are not real shoals compared with that hell gate of Kongling Shoal". Twenty-four reefs, named Great Pearl, First Pearl, Second Pearl, Third Pearl, etc., are crammed in the shoal, bulging into each other's way. The Great Pearl, for example, sprawls in the middle of the river, dividing it into two channels, the south channel full of jagged reefs and fickle eddies, the north narrow, twisted, and forbidding with submerged rocks. Besides, there was a hideous reef called "Coming-at-Me", which used to fill people with fear. This is a shoal where passing boats had to thread their way through the reefs, dodging from side to side all the time.

After liberation, however, rocks were blasted away and waterways were dredged to make these shoals less dangerous, and especially with the accomplishment of the Gezhouba Dam, the water level is higher now, and the earlier dreadful gorges have become easy of access.

晨光秀色 Charming landscape in the morning sun.

崆嶺峽
Kongling Gorge..

黃　陵　廟

　　黃陵廟位於長江南岸黃牛岩下九龍山麓正中，背依山岩，前臨大江，掩映在香柑金桔林中，是三峽中最大最古老的建築。

　　相傳黃陵廟始建於春秋時代，原叫黃牛廟。三國時諸葛亮率師入蜀，途經黃牛峽，看到此廟已破爛不堪，便親自主持重建，并寫下膾炙人口的《黃陵廟記》，後人把它刻碑珍藏於廟，尊爲"武侯碑"。

　　黃陵廟內供奉大禹像，相傳遠古時候，大禹率衆來此治水，因高山阻擋，八年難以疏通，百姓深受水災之害。土星被感動，變成一頭勇猛的黃牛，觸開高山，犁出峽道，助禹治水成功，并深愛這裏的百姓和山水草木，化成了一座高入雲端的黃牛岩。

　　黃牛岩高千餘米，霞光之中，遠看好像一幅畫：一位粗黑的壯士牽着一頭牛，正昂首向前。

　　黃陵廟與黃牛岩吸引着歷代文人墨客，歐陽修、蘇東坡、陳子昂、李白、白居易、劉禹錫等都在這裏留下了足跡，寫下了許多千古流傳的詩篇。

HUANGLING TEMPLE

Huangling Temple, the biggest and the oldest building in the Yangtze Gorges, is located right at the foot of the Nine Dragons Hill in front of the Ox Rock on the south bank. Backed by the huge mountain rocks and facing the river, it sits in a garden of fragrant golden oranges.

The story has it that Huangling Temple was first built in the Spring and Autumn Period (770～476 B. C.) and named Huangniu Temple (the Ox Temple). In the Three Kingdoms Period (220～265), when Zhuge Liang passed the temple, leading his troops on their way to Shu (one of the kingdoms) and saw it on the verge of collapse, he stopped over and put himself in charge of the renovation. It was here that he wrote the admirable essay *Hungling Temple*, which was later inscribed on a stele, worshipped as the "Wuhou Stele".

Enshrined in the temple is the statue of Yu the Great. The legend goes that in ancient times, Yu was here leading the people in their fight against floods. But for eight long years they could not find an outlet for the floods, which were always blocked by the mountains. As a result, the local people were constantly harassed by floods. The god Tuxing was so much moved by Yu's unremitting efforts that he turned into a valiant ox, gored the mountain apart, and ploughed up a gorge, thus helping to fulfil Yu's task. Then, reluctant to leave the local people and the land that he had come to love so much, the god changed into the sky-high Ox Rock.

The Ox Rock is over 1,000m high. Seen from a distance in the sun rays, it looks like a dusky statue of a sturdy man heroically leading an ox forward.

Throughout the ages, Huangling Temple and the Ox Rock have attracted many literary men. Famous writers and poets such as Ouyang Xiu, Su Shi, Chen Zi'ang, Li Bai, and Liu Yuxi visited this place and bequeathed a number of excellent poems, which will be handed down forever.

2		
1	3	

1　三斗坪
Sandouping.

2　黃牛峽
Huangniu Gorge.

3　黃陵廟
Huangling Temple.

西陵晚霞
Xiling Gorge in sunset glow.

春雪
Spring snow.

西陵峡春色
Spring scene
in Xiling Gorge.

九龍過江
Nine dragons crossing river.

南沱 "三把刀"
Three Swords at Nantuo.

涉險 "天生橋" Venturing on Heavenly Bridge.

險奇的西陵峽
Dangerous and quaint Xiling Gorge.

馬鈴巖
Horse-Bell Rock

石牌青獅
Mt. Qingshi in Shipai Town.

南 津 關

南津關位於西陵峽東口，"三峽至此窮"，爲三峽尾端的天然門戶。

南津關北岸的下牢溪，傳說劉備曾派兵在此駐守，至今尚有劉封城和張飛擂鼓台遺址。南津關兩岸地勢險要，陡壁直立，江面狹窄，猶如細頸瓶口，鎖住滔滔大江，"雄關蜀道，巍鎮荆門"，歷來爲兵家必爭之地。

長江一出南津關，便急劇南折，兩岸山勢坦蕩，江面驟然變寬，江流由飛旋洶湧而漸趨平緩。關口內外，景色迥異。如果是出峽，便會使人有"送盡奇峰雙眼豁，江天空闊而夷陵"之感。

THE NANJINGUAN PASS

"The Yangtze Gorges ends at the Nanjinguan Pass." Situated at the eastern end of Xiling Gorge. the Nanjinguan Pass is the natural exit of the Gorges.

It is said that Liu Bei (king of Shu) once posted his troops there to garrison the pass. Today we can still see the relics of Liu Bei's fortress and the spot where Zhang Fei (a general under Liu) beat the drum. As sheer cliffs close in on the river. the Nanjinguan Pass banks are difficult of access. It is like the narrow neck of a flask curbing the mighty Yangtze waters. "Impregnable Shu pass. garrison of Jingmen Gate". the pass was a strategic point all through the ages.

Rushing out of the Nanjinguan Pass. the Yangtze bends sharply southward. Then the mountains stretch away and the river widens abruptly. the surging. whirling waters calmed down. The landscape varies drastically in and out of the pass.

Cruising out. one experiences the sensation described in a poem:

Sending off peaks so spectacular,
I am greeted by the open sky and water.
The river is so vast and the horizon so far,
That the mountains seem all razed.

南津關 Nanjinguan Pass.

變化奇妙的三峽水

三峽之險，不僅表現在陡岩峭壁、急流險灘上，而且還表現在令人望而生畏、變化奇妙的險水上。那由水底向水面翻湧、宛如沸騰的開水的泡水，那旋轉不止並集於一點的淡水，那翻騰着朵朵水花的花水，以及奇形怪狀的橫流水、眉毛水、跌水等，在江面上時隱時現，此起彼伏，變化無窮，使你眼花繚亂，情趣橫生。

FICKLE AND MIRACULOUS WATERS

The danger of the Yangtze Gorges is found not only in the precipitous cliffs and jagged crags, but also in the treacherous waters that daunt people at first glance with its miraculous changes. The bubbles welling up from the riverbed like boiling water, the eddies that whirl on and on at one spot, the sprays that splash and splatter about wildly, as well as the curious crossing current, the brow-shaped flow, and the tumbling torrent all on and off, one after another, full of changes, always dazzle the spellbound tourists and have added greatly to the charm of the Yangtze Gorges.

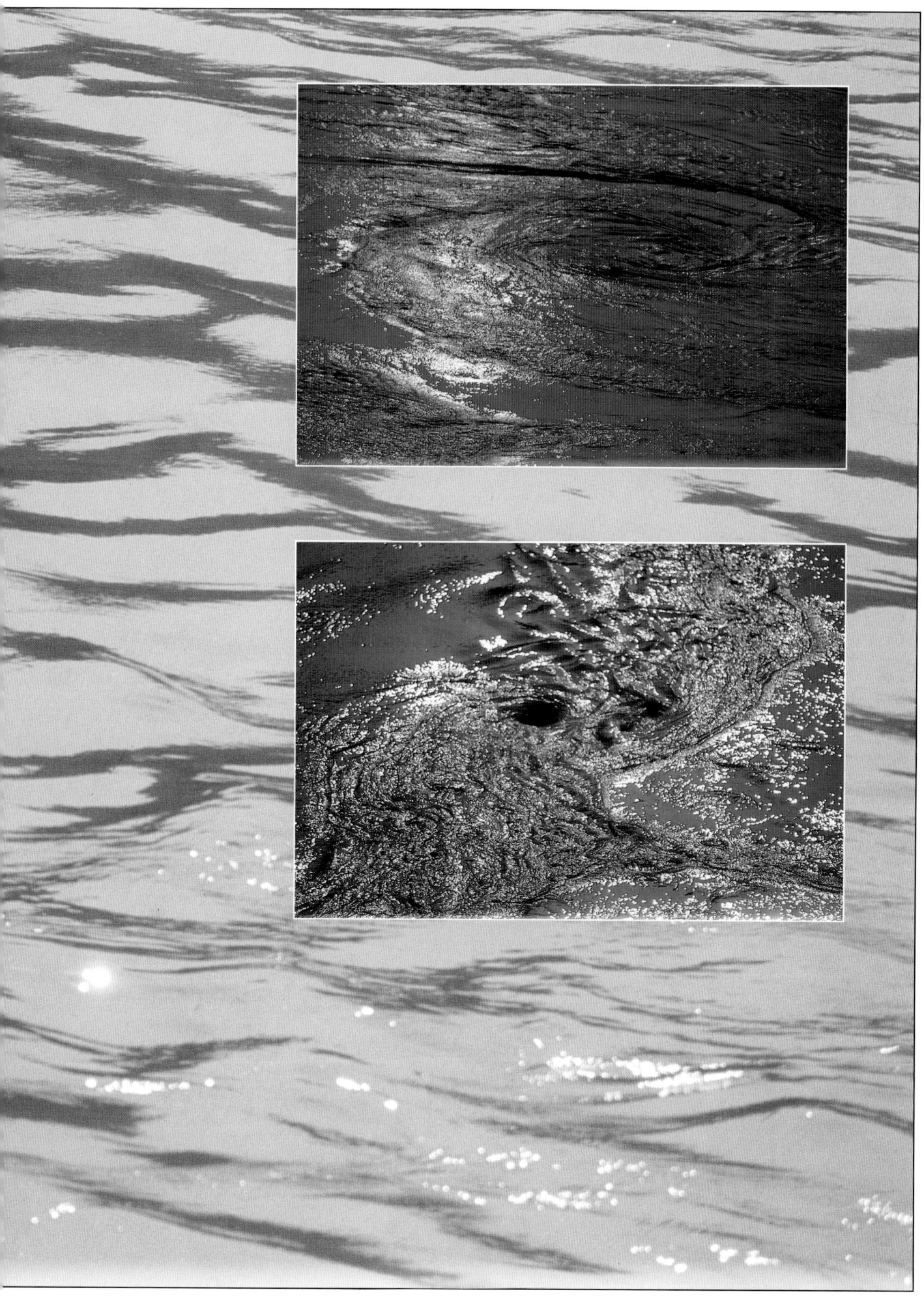

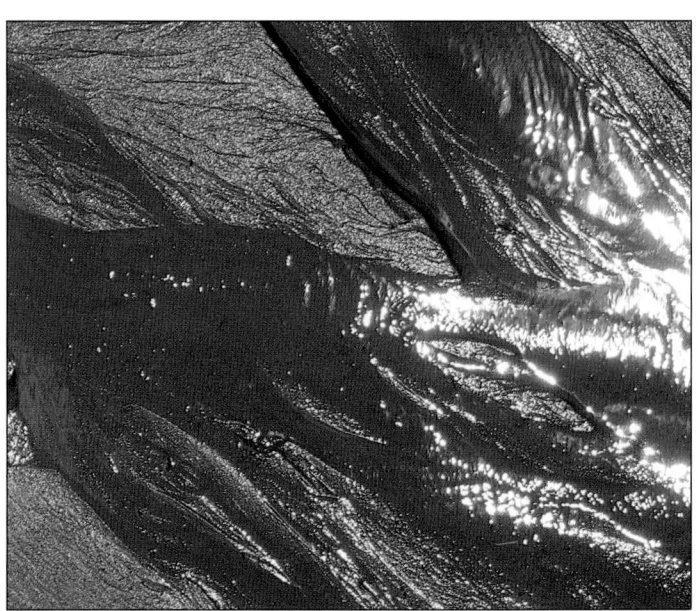

三峽溶洞奇觀

"怪怪與奇奇，萬狀不可名。"

三峽溶洞有200多個，其中絕大部分分佈在石灰岩特別多的西陵峽中。這些洞分佈在兩岸山崖上，有的臨近水旁，有的處於山腰，有的高踞山頂。洞內流水潺潺，迂迴曲折，乳石橫生，千奇百怪，萬千景象。

位於瞿塘峽北岸絕壁山腰上的七道門溶洞，洞深曲折，洞中有洞，景中有景，景色奇異。洞寬處大如廣場，洞窄處僅能容一人側身通過。洞中怪石嵯峨，各種石筍石乳千姿百態，琳瑯滿目。在二道門頂端，有一天窗面對大江，從這裏眺望夔峽江天，雲天一綫，妙不可言。

位於巫峽與大寧河交滙處北岸的陸游洞，因陸游曾在此夜宿而得名。由清水洞、金柱洞、玉林洞交錯組成，相連貫通，各具特色，融洞景峽景於一體。清水洞寬敞高大，四壁如刀削斧劈，洞頂石乳高低錯落，燈光中如繁星點點；金柱洞由一條長10米寬5米的長廊組成，洞內有20米高的乳白色石柱，由洞底直插洞頂，氣勢磅礴，柱身玲瓏剔透，名曰"金柱撐天"。

燕子阡溶洞位於神農溪鸚鵡峽西岸，洞高80米，寬30米，洞深5公里，呈長方形，好似張開大嘴的河馬。洞內棲息着成千上萬的珍禽——短嘴金絲燕，故名燕子阡。洞內上有燕子飛舞，下有流水潺潺，岩溶堆積，宛如層層梯田。

三遊洞位於宜昌市西北郊西陵山的峭壁上，面臨清澈的下牢溪。相傳唐元和十四年（公元819年），白居易與其弟白行簡和詩人元稹相約同遊此洞，各賦詩20韻刻於壁上，由白居易作《三遊洞序》："以吾三人始遊，故曰爲三遊洞。"到了宋代，著名文學家蘇洵、蘇軾、蘇轍，慕名同遊三遊洞，也各題詩一首，刻於壁上。後人稱白居易等三人之遊爲"前三遊"，蘇軾父子之遊爲"後三遊"。洞中鐘乳石、石筍和石柱比比皆是，千姿百態，妙狀難名。洞分前後兩室，前室明曠，題刻滿壁；後室幽暗，奧妙莫測。洞內頂部原有石鐘二處，以石擊之，其聲如鐘；石子落地，其響如鼓，故有"天鐘地鼓"之說。洞中還保存有各種題刻、壁畫等古文物。

金獅洞位於宜昌市郊的長江北岸，因入洞口處有一巨型乳石形如雄獅而得名。金獅洞是距今約100萬年的石灰岩溶洞，洞深1585米，洞內千奇百怪、瑩光明潤的鐘乳石及種種石灰質結構，造成了一個規模宏大的地下宮殿，展現出一個由具體的景觀與想象和幻覺交織而成的神話世界。

KARST GROTTO WONDERS IN THE YANGTZE GORGES

Ten thousand shapes beyond description,
Each more grotesque and bizarre than the other.

There are more than 200 karst grottoes in the Yangtze Gorges region, mainly distributed along Xiling Gorge, an area abundant in limestone. These grottoes are scattered on the cliffs on either bank—some close to the river, some halfway up, and some high up right on the top. In the grottoes, small streams murmur around the twists and turns. Stalactites and stalagmites are everywhere in multifarious shapes. A scene of wonders indeed.

Seven Gates, a karst grotto halfway up the cliff on the north bank at Qutang Gorge, is very deep, where a winding path leads into one grotto after another. There are grottoes inside grottoes and karst scenes over karst scenes, all unique and spectacular. The grottoes may be as spacious as a plaza and may be so small that one has to sidle through. The limestones are steep, sharp and peculiar, and the display of stalactites and stalagmites of all shapes is a feast for the eyes. On the top of the second gate, facing the river, there is a skylight, where one can look into the distance at Kui Gorge, a scene of the river, and the clouds too beautiful for words.

Lu You Grotto, so named because Lu You (great poet of the Song Dynasty) had once stayed in it overnight, is situated on the north bank where the Daning River runs into Wu Gorge. It consists of three small caves—Qingshui, Jinzhu, and Yulin—connected in a crisscross pattern, each with its own distinctive features. Here the landscape of the gorge and the grotto sights interplay in a harmonious whole. The spacious Qingshui Grotto has walls that seem to have been cut out with a sword. When the grotto is lit up, the stalactites hanging from overhead, high and low at random, look like many stars strewn across the night sky. Another cave, Jinzhu (Golden Pillar), is actually a passage 10m long and 5m wide. A 20m-high cream-coloured karst column, exquisitely sculptured by nature, rises sheer out of the ground and up to the roof with great momentum. This sight is known as "Golden Pillar Propping the Sky".

The Swallow Path, a rectangular karst grotto on the west bank of Parrot Gorge on the Shennong River, 80m high, 30m wide, and 5km deep, looks like a yawning hippopotamus. In it live thousands and thousands of short-billed collocalias, rare birds of the swallow kind. Hence the name Swallow Path. Here swallows flit high and low over a murmuring stream-and the heaped karst, which resembles terraced fields.

Facing the limpid Xialao Stream, Three Tourists Grotto is in the cliff of Mt. Xiling in the northwest suburbs of Yichang City. The story goes that in the year of 819, the well-known poet Bai Juyi, his brother Bai Xingjian, and another famous poet Yuan Zhen visited this cave together. Each of them composed a 20-rhyme poem and inscribed it on the wall, and Bai Juyi wrote the *Preface to The Three Tourists*, in which he claimed, "as we are the first three tourists here, we hereby name the cave Three Tourists". Later on, the famous Song Dynasty literary men Su Xun (father), Su Shi and Su Zhe (sons) came to visit the cave out of admiration. They each wrote a poem, too, and inscribed them on the wall. Since then the first group have been referred to as "the earlier three tourists", and the Sus as "the later three tourists". In the grotto, the ubiquitous stalactites, stalagmites and karst columns present a variety of indescribably grotesque shapes. The grotto is divided into a front cave and a back cave—the front one bright and spacious, its walls full of inscriptions, and the back one dark and mysterious. There used to be two karst bells hanging from the roof. When hit by a stone, they sounded like bells; when the stone fell onto the ground, there was the thundering of a drum. Hence the name "Heaven Bells and Earth Drums". There are also valuable antiquities, such as various inscriptions and mural paintings, kept in the grotto.

The Golden Lion Grotto lies on the north bank in the suburbs of Yichang City, so named because of the huge lionlike stalactite at the entrance. The grotto is 1,585m deep and 1,000,000 years old. The gleaming, moist stalactites of all fantastic shapes and various stalactic structures make a grand subterranean palace of the cave, thus displaying a mythological world—a combination of real sights, imagination and visions.

巫峽陸游洞

Lu You Grotto in Wu Gorge.

1 溶洞
  Karst cave.

2 世界上最大的天坑——奉節小寨天坑
  Xiaozhai Natural Pit, world's largest.

3 神農溪燕子阡洞
  Swallow Path on Shennongxi River.

4 西陵峽溶洞景觀
  Karst cave scene in Xiling Gorge.

5 金獅洞
  Golden Lion Cave.

三遊洞石壁古代題刻
Ancient rock engravings
in Three Tourists Grotto.

三遊洞
Three Tourists Grotto.

萬里長江第一壩

萬里長江第一壩──葛洲壩水利樞紐工程，橫跨在南津關前３公里處寬闊的大江之上。

葛洲壩全長2561米，高達70米。葛洲壩水利樞紐主要建築有發電站、船閘、泄水閘、衝沙閘、防淤堤等。二座電站分別在大江、二江，總裝機容量271萬5千千瓦，年平均發電138億度。三座船閘，其中一、二號船閘閘室寬34米，長280米，可通過萬噸級客貨輪和大型船隊，是目前世界上最大的船閘之一。27孔泄水閘和12孔衝沙閘，每秒鐘可宣泄11萬立方米的洪水，即使遇到特大洪水，也能安全泄洪。

雄偉壯觀的葛洲壩水利樞紐工程具有發電、通航、泄洪等綜合功能，它像一顆燦爛的明珠，閃爍在萬里長江之上，爲美麗雄偉的三峽增添了新的異彩。

與葛洲壩水利樞紐相連的宜昌市，"控楚蜀之交帶，當水陸之要衝"，素有川鄂咽喉之稱，是長江上、中游的中轉港。葛洲壩水利樞紐工程的興建，大大推動了宜昌的城市建設和工業的發展，使這座歷史古城面貌煥然一新，成爲水電新城。宜昌山青水秀，風景優美，名勝古跡除享有盛名的葛洲壩和三遊洞外，還有清幽典雅的爾雅書院和巍峨壯觀、風鈴悅耳的天然塔等。

THE FIRST DAM ON THE YANGTZE RIVER

The first dam on the Yangtze — Gezhouba Key Water Control Project — runs across the broad section of the river 3km down the Nanjinguan Pass.

The dam is 2.561m long and 70m high. The project is made up of three parts, Dajiang, Erjang and Sanjiang, consisting of hydro-power stations, ship locks, sluice gates, scouring sluices and anti-silt dykes. The two hydro-power stations are built on Dajiang with a total installed capacity of 2,715,000km and an annual electric energy production of 13.8kwh. There are three ship locks. The passages of No. 1 and No. 2 locks are 34m in breadth and 280m in length, large enough for 10,000-ton-class passengers and cargo ships or a large fleet to get by. It is one of the largest ship locks in the world. The 27-tunneled sluice gate and the 12-arched scouring sluice can drain off 110,000 cubic metres of floodwater every second. They can let out a catastrophic flood without any danger.

The magnificent project has a comprehensive function of power generating, navigation, flood discharge and so on. Like a bright pearl, it gives off ever-lasting brilliance on the long river, adding a special charm to the Yangtze Gorges.

Yichang City, which is close to Gezhouba Key Water Control Project, is regarded as the throat of Sichuan and Hubei Provinces, being a hub of water and land communications and a transfer port in the upper and lower reaches of the Yangtze River. This project has greatly accelerated the urban construction and the development of the industry in Yichang City, and, consequently, the ancient city has taken on a completely new look and become a modern city of hydro-power. Besides the giant dam, Yichang boasts a lot of scenic and historical spots. Among them are Three Tourists Grotto, Erya Classical Learning Academy, which is antique and elegant, and Natural Pagoda, which is magnificent, with the aeolian bells pleasing to the ear.

葛洲壩水利樞紐鳥瞰
Bird's-eye view of Gezhouba Key Water Control Project.

泄洪闸
The sluice gate.

船闸
The ship lock.

三峽是川鄂兩省人民生活的地方，這裏主要居住着漢族和土家族，他們有着許多獨特的風俗和習慣。這裏還是國寶中華鱘的生息之地，龍舟競渡的聖地，萬紫千紅的水果生產基地。來到三峽，你能處處領略到濃郁而多彩的民族風情。

在奉節，你可看到熱鬧的人日踏磧活動，它是夔州百姓的傳統風俗。每年正月初七人日這天，男女老少懷着對諸葛亮的敬仰，穿紅著綠，成羣結隊出遊諸葛亮排八陣圖的磧上。人們在磧上鳴鼓奏樂，載歌載舞。婦女們在磧上挑揀些五彩斑斕的石子，用五彩絲綾穿幷在一起，繫於釵頭，或戴在小孩身上，用它來興吉避邪。

在巴東，你可看到一個背簍世界。因三峽城鎮大多依山臨江，街道陡斜，居民上下唯有步行。在街上，在山路邊，男女老少身後都揹着一個背簍或是一個木架子，或是揹着貨物，或是揹着一個小孩。行走時以木杖助力，休息時以木杖支撐竹簍。此情此景，別有情趣。

在土家族居住地，你可看到那獨特的婚俗、喪俗。新娘出嫁前要哭半月，由人揹送轎上。喪俗即跳喪舞，靈前置一大鼓，一人擊鼓，數人對舞，擊鼓者領唱，舞者邊舞邊唱，唱腔高亢粗獷。

在秭歸，你可看到那熱火朝天的龍舟賽。每年農曆五月初五龍舟賽，是楚鄉人民爲表達對屈原的崇敬而舉行的一種祭禮活動。屆時，龍舟競發，浪花飛濺，蕩槳聲、鑼鼓聲、號子聲，滙成一曲高亢激昂的交響樂。

此外，你還可到清澈碧透的香溪，去尋覓那形狀如傘、乳白透明的桃花魚；到古樸的巫山水口鎮，去品嘗那細如髮絲、味道鮮美的水口掛面；到波濤洶湧的江流中，觀賞那被稱作魚類之冠、神態威武的國寶——中華鱘；到沿岸那五彩繽紛的柑桔園中，品嘗芬芳，擷取詩情……

THE FOLKWAYS OF THE GORGE REGION

The region of the Yangtze Gorge is populated by a large number of Han and Tujia people of Sichuan and Hubei Provinces with various unique customs and folkways. It is also a place for the Chinese sturgeon, a national treasure of China, to propagate and the birthplace of the dragon boat race, which is so popular in China, as well as in the other countries and regions of Asia. What's more, it is a base of fruit production. Everywhere in the region you may enjoy yourself with the colourful folkways and customs characteristic of the ethnical flavour.

In Fengjie you may happen to see the exciting scene of the commemoration of the Eight-Element Battle Formation designed by Zhuge Liang during the period of the Three Kingdoms. The commemoration is a traditional folk-activity of Kuizhou. On the seventh day of the first moon every year men and women, old and young, all in their best, gather on the beach, which is the former site of Zhuge Liang's Eight-Element Battle Formation, beating gongs and drums, singing and dancing heartily. Women pick up colourful fine pebbles and string them up with coloured silk thread and then wear the string on their hairpins or around the necks of the children to ensure good luck.

In Badong you will see a world of baskets carried on the back. Since the towns and walled cities of the gorge region are mostly situated on riverside mountains, the streets are oblique or even steep. The citizens can only get about on foot. In a street or on a path you may come across men and women, old and young, who carry a basket or a wooden rack with goods or a little child in it. While walking they have a stick to support themselves and while resting they have the stick to support the baskets. The scene is really of exotic flavour.

In a Tujia dwelling place, you may get some idea of the unique wedding and funeral customs. As to the former the most unique is that before she is married off, a bride has to force a weep for half a month until she is carried on the back and put into a sedan-chair. The funeral custom, on the other hand, is characterised by the funeral dance: a big drum is set before the coffin and a man beats the drum while others dance. The man leads a chorus and the others sing loudly in an unconstrained manner.

In Zigui you see the rousing scene of the dragon boat race. On the fifth day of the fifth moon every year, the people of Chu Township hold a memorial ceremony to express their great reverence for Qu Yuan, a great poet of Chu State. At the time hundreds of boats compete with one another, water spraying, oars paddling and drums and gongs resounding to the skies, making a sonorous symphony.

Besides, you may go to the Xiangxi River to look for the minnows which are cream-coloured and transparent in the shape of an umbrella, to Shuikou Township in Wushan to taste the delicious noodles as thin as hair, to the surging Yangtze River to view and admire the powerful-looking Chinese sturgeons, a national treasure of China, and to orange and tangerine orchards by the river to enjoy the fragrance and refresh your poetic inspiration...

光與影　Light and shadow.

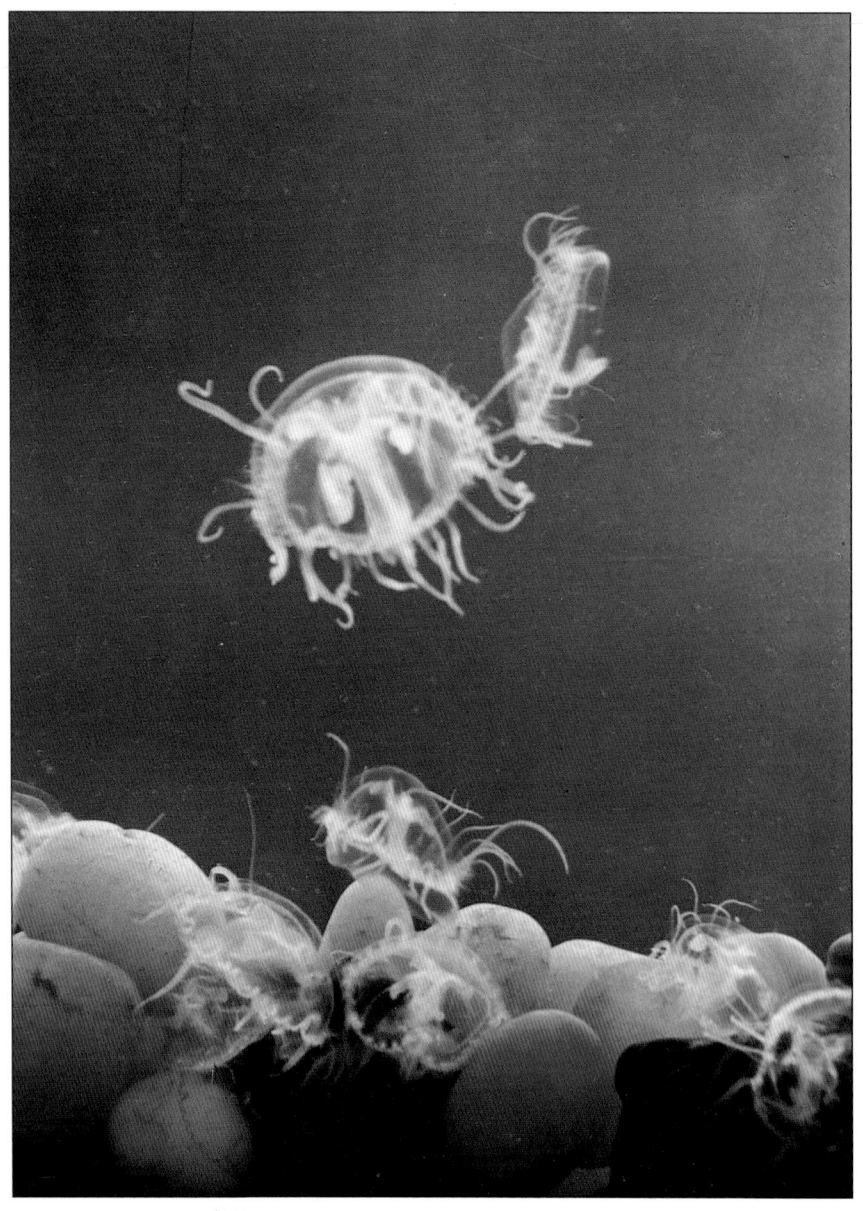

桃花魚，又名桃花水母，每至桃花盛開時節，一簇簇桃花魚，一閃一閃地蕩漾在碧波裏，仿佛在與岸上的桃花相媲美。當桃花凋謝時，它也隨花消逝，故名桃花魚。

Minnow.called " Peach fish" in Chinese, come in schools when peach trees are in blossom. They glisten in the limpid river, as if rivaling peach blossoms on the banks in beauty. They disappear with the withering of the peach blossoms. Hence the name.

巫峽夜泊　Night mooring at Wu Gorge.

峽岸牧羊　Tending sheep on the bank

三峽猴　Monkeys of the Gorge region.

輕舟晚唱　Eventide skiff.

Chinese sturgeon.

The Chinese sturgeon is mainly distributed in the trunk tributaries of the Yangtze River and some coastal rivers. Between summer and autumn every year, they swim in schools upstream to the Jinsha River, where they spawn. After their young are bred, they all swim downstream to grow in the East Sea and the Yellow Sea. The Chinese sturgeon is large in size and imposing and dignified in bearing. A grown-up Chinese sturgeon can reach over 4m in length and over one thousand pounds in weight, ranking the biggest of all the 27 sturgeons in the world. It is among the government-protected aquatic animals.

中華鱘，主要分佈於長江干流和沿海水域，每年夏秋，成羣溯江而上，到金沙江一帶產卵；繁殖後順流而下，到東海、黃海育肥成長。它個體碩大，形態威武，成年中華鱘體長可達四米多，體重超過千斤，爲世界二十七種鱘魚之冠。是我國重點保護的水生動物。

峡江小渡　Gorge ferry.　　　　待渡 "小餐"　A snack before ferry.

纤夫　Boat trackers.

編織　Weaving.

寧河之晨　Morning of the Ninghe River.

龍昌渡口　Longchang Ferry.

高山小吊樓　Ever-Hanging house.

晚歸　Returning in the dusk.

三峡廣柑，三峡是我國著名的柑桔產地之一。僅以屈原的《桔頌》為據，三峡栽培柑桔的歷史就有兩千多年。如今峡江兩岸都郁蔥蔥的柑桔樹上，金黃赤紅的菓實掛滿枝頭，給雄姿險峻的三峡，又添上了美麗富饒的色彩。

Yangtze Gorges tangerine The Gorges region tangerine is one of the well-known tangerine growing areas in China. Qu Yuan's Ode to Tangerines has borne out the fact that tangerines were grown in the area at least 2,000 years ago. Now, the luxuriant tangerine and orange trees on either bank, laden with golden and red fruits, add a touch of beautiful abundance to the scene of magnificence and peril in the gorges.

山寨人家
Mountain village household.

獼猴桃
Chinese gooseberry (actinidia chinensis).

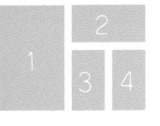

冬雪千坵
Drifts of winter snow.

巴東風情
Badong folkways.

長階小巷
　Long flight **in** little lane

滿載而歸
　Back from a fruitful journey.

巴人祭火
Local fire-worshipping ceremony.

包粽子　Making Zongzi.

土家族婚俗——交杯酒　Mutual toasting—a Tujia wedding custom.

龍舟競渡　Racing dragon boats.

峡江光影
Shadow playing on the river

三峽是全國重點旅遊綫之一。爲了讓中外遊客飽覽三峽風光，以中國長江輪船總公司爲核心的中國長江航運集團，不僅開闢了客運兼旅遊的普通客輪航綫（乘坐此輪，旅客既可觀賞峽內風光，又可登岸參觀沿岸名勝古跡），還開闢了豪華型旅遊船航綫，成立了專業化的長江輪船海外旅遊總公司，擁有崑崙、神女、三峽、峨嵋、巴山、西陵、隆中、白帝、長江之星、長江明珠、長江公主等十多艘符合國際水準，又具中國特色的豪華、高級旅遊船。遊船集吃、住、行、遊、娛、購於一體，服務週到，生活舒適，堪稱水上樂園。

此外，長江上游段各地方航運公司也開闢了中小型客輪航綫。現在，武漢至重慶，宜昌至重慶，宜昌至奉節，每天都有大中小型客輪上下，是遊覽三峽的主要交通工具。

The Yangtze Gorges is one of the key tourist lines of the country. In order that tourists from home and abroad can enjoy the scenery of the Yangtze Gorges, Changjiang National Shipping Blocl, headed by Changjiang National Shipping Corporation, has opened up a shipping line for ordinary and luxury cruise liners as well as passenger ships. Aboard you can view all the gorge landscapes and ashore you can visit the scenic and historical sites along the river. Changjiang National Overseas Shipping Tourist Corporation possesses more than ten high-graded and luxury cruise liners such as *Kunlun*, *Shennu*, *Sanxia*, *Emei*, *Bashan*, *Xiling*, *Longzhong*, *Baidi*, *Star of the Yangtze*, *Bright Pearl of the Yangtze*, *and Princess of Yangtze*, which are all up to international standards and of the distinctive Chinese national features. The ships include the service of the basic necessities of life as well as shopping and recreation. They are regarded as paradise on water for their good service and comfortable accommodations.

In addition local shipping companies have opened up lines for the small and medium-sized tourist ships.

Every day ships of different sizes sail up and down the river from Wuhan to Chongqing, from Yichang to Chongqing and from Yichang to Fengjie. They are the main means of transportation for Yangtze Gorges tour.

三峽古詩選

● 瞿塘峽

早發白帝城

（唐）李白

朝辭白帝彩雲間，
千里江陵一日還。
兩岸猿聲啼不住，
輕舟已過萬重山。

長江

（唐）杜甫

眾水會涪萬，瞿塘爭一門。
朝宗人共挹，盜賊爾誰尊？
孤石隱如馬，高蘿垂飲猿。
歸心異波浪，何事即飛翻。

竹枝詞

（唐）白居易

瞿塘峽口冷烟低，
白帝城頭月向西。
唱到竹枝聲咽處，
寒猿闇鳥一時啼。

瞿塘峽

（清）張問陶

峽雨蒙蒙竟日閒，
扁舟真落畫圖間。
縱將萬管玲瓏筆，
難寫瞿塘兩岸山。

白鹽赤甲

（清）張問陶

白鹽雲外落，赤甲雨中蟠。
峽坼天光細，山童石氣完。
關河夔府秀，疏鑿禹功難。
孤艇愁風雪，飄飄逼歲寒。

峽門秋月

（清）張宗世

燭龍不照古陰崖，
偏有明蟾度嶺來。
三峽憑將秋送人，
雙門似背月推開。
當關以望珠懸闕，
排洇而登鏡在台。
好景一年剛一見，
莫辭風露立蒼臺。

夔州歌十絕句（選二）

（唐）杜甫

中巴之東巴東山，
江水開闢流其間。
白帝高為三峽鎮，
瞿塘險過百牢關。

赤甲白鹽俱刺天，
閭閻繚繞接山巔。
楓林桔樹丹青合，
復道重樓錦繡懸。

峽中鐵柱

（元）何同男

白帝城邊春草生，
黃牛峽裏水波清。
追思昭烈千年事，
長使英雄氣不平。

夔州竹枝歌九首（選一）

（南宋）范成大

赤甲白鹽碧叢叢，
半山人家草木風。
榴花滿山紅似火，
荔子天凉未肯紅。

● 巫峽

三峽歌

（宋）陸游

十二巫山見九峰，
船頭彩翠滿秋空。
朝雲暮雨渾虛語，
一夜猿啼明月中。

巫峽

（清）張問陶

雲點巫山洞壑重，
參天亂插碧芙蓉。
可憐十二奇峰外，
更有零星百萬峰。

巫山高

（唐）李端

巫山十二峰，皆在碧虛中。
迴合雲藏日，霏微雨帶風。
猿聲寒度水，樹色暮連空。
愁向高唐去，清秋見楚宮。

巫山曲

（唐）孟郊

巴江上峽重復重，
陽台碧峭十二峰。
荆王獵時逢暮雨，
夜臥高丘夢神女。
輕紅流烟濕艷姿，
行雲飛去明星稀。
目極魂斷望不見，
猿啼三聲淚滴衣。

過巫峽

（唐）李頻

擁棹向驚湍，巫峰直上看。
削成從水底，聳出在雲端。
暮雨晴時少，啼猿渴下難。
一聞神女去，鳳竹掃空壇。

過楚宮

（唐）李商隱

巫峽迢迢舊楚宮，
至今雲雨暗丹楓。
微生盡戀人間樂，
祇有襄王憶夢中。

巫山道中

（明）黃輝

未曾五里巴三溪，
幾許寒崖掛斷霓。
亂石疊成春雪碓，
斷橋橫作上天梯。

神女廟

（唐）劉禹錫

巫山十二鬱蒼蒼，
片石亭亭號女郎。
曉霧乍開疑捲幔，
山花欲謝似殘妝。
星河好夜聞清風，
雲雨歸時帶異香。
何事神仙九天上，
人間來就楚襄王。

即事

（唐）杜甫

暮春三峽巫峽長，
晶晶行雲浮日光。
雷聲忽送千峰雨，
花氣渾如百和香。
黃鶯過水翻迴去，
燕子啣泥濕不妨。
飛閣捲簾圖畫裏，
虛無祇少對瀟湘。

夜雨寄北

（唐）李商隱

君問歸期未有期，
巴山夜雨漲秋池。
何當共翦西窗燭，
卻話巴山夜雨時。

● 西陵峽

上三峽

（唐）李白

巫山夾青天，巴水流若茲。
巴水忽可盡，青天無到時。
三朝上黃牛，三暮行太遲。
三朝又三暮，不覺鬢成絲。

黃牛峽

（清）張問陶

好奇須過古巴東，
千水千山貌不同。
看到黃牛三峽盡，
可憐丘壑滿胸中。

過東灘入馬肺峽

（宋）陸游

船上急灘如退鷁，
人緣絕壁似飛猱。
口誇遠嶺青千峰，
心憶平波綠一篙。

扇子峽

（宋）陸游

不肯爬沙桂樹邊，
柔頤千古向岩前。
巴東峽裏最初峽，
天下泉中第四泉。
嚙雪飲冰疑換骨，
掬球弄月可忘年。
清遊自笑何曾足，
疊鼓咚咚又解船。

初入峽有感

（唐）白居易

上有萬仞山，
下有千丈水。
蒼蒼兩崖間，
闊峽容一葦。

入崆嶺峽

（清）劉肇紳

峽壁千尋並，
羣峰一綫開。
江聲呼岸走，
山影壓船來。

初入峽山效孟東野

（南宋）范成大

峽山偪而峻，峽泉湍似琦。
峽草如毬毛，峽樹多摎枝。
峽禽惟杜鵑，血吻日夜嗁。
峽馬類黃狗，不能長鳴嘶。
峽曉虎跡多，峽暮人跡稀。
峽路如登天，猿鶴不敢梯。
僕夫負崌哭，我亦呻吟悲。
悲吟不成章，聊賡峽哀詩。

過黃牛峽

（唐）張蠙

黃牛來勢瀉巴川，
疊日孤舟逐峽前。
雷電夜驚猿落樹，
波濤愁恐客離船。
盤渦逆入嵌空地，
斷壁高分繚繞天。
多少人經過此去，
一生魂夢泊灤淺。

新灘

（宋）蘇軾

扁舟轉山曲，未至已先驚。
白浪橫江起，槎牙似雪城。
番番從高來，一一投澗坑。
大魚不能上，暴腮灘下橫。
小魚散復合，瀺灂如遭烹。
鱞鰍不敢下，飛過兩翅輕。
白鷺夸瘦捷，插腳還欲傾。
區區舟上人，薄技安敢呈。
祇應灘頭廟，賴此牛酒盈。

竹枝歌

（明）揚升庵

無義灘頭風浪收，
黃牛開處見黃牛。
白波一道青峰裏，
聽盡猿聲是峽州。

長江沿綫風光名勝

　　遊覽完雄奇秀美的三峽，人們還可從此出發，飽覽大江上下的無限風光。從夔峽溯江而上，可目睹石寶寨、酆都鬼城、山城重慶的豐采。在西陵峽順江而下，可觀賞荆州古城，湖南的岳陽樓，武漢的黃鶴樓，九江的廬山，彭澤小孤山，安徽的九華山、黃山，南京的中山陵、鎮江塔，南通的狼山和上海市容、浦江風光。

SCENIC BEAUTIES
ALONG THE YANGTZE

　　Having cruised through the magnificent and beautiful Yangtze Gorges, you can start a new sightseeing tour to enjoy the beautifullandscape along the river. Sailing upstream from Kui Gorge, you will admire the Shibaozhai Village, the Fengdu Ghost City, and Chongqing, the mountainside city; floating downstream from Xiling Gorge, you will be able to see the ancient city of Jingzhou, the Yueyang Tower in Hunan, the Huanghe (Yellow Crane) Tower in Wuhan, Mt. Lushan in Jiujiang, the Xiaogushan Island in Pengze, Mt. Jiuhua in Anhui, the Sun Yetsen Mausoleum and the Zhenjiang Tower in Nanjing, Mt. Langshan in Nantong, etc., and to go sightseeing in Shanghai and on the Huangpu River.

瞿塘峽
Qutang Gorge

巫峽
Wu Gorge

西陵峽
Xiling Gorge

奉節
Fengjie

萬縣
Wanxian

巴東
Badong

宜昌
Yichang

酆都
Fengdu

重慶
Chongqing

洞庭湖
Lake Dong

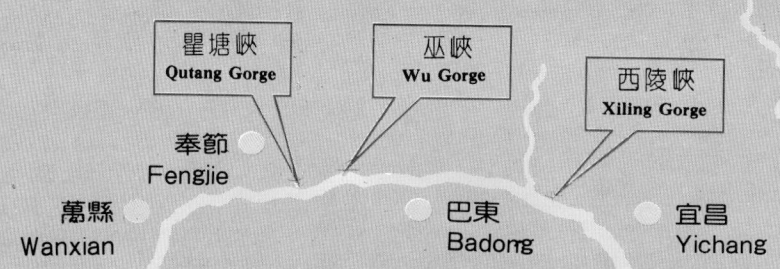

▲重庆之夜　Night Scene in Chongqing

▲鬼城　Ghost City

▲石宝寨　Shibaozhai

▲岳阳楼　Yueyang Tower

▲黄鹤楼 Yellow Crane Tower

南京
Nanjing

上海
Shanghai

蕪湖
Wuhu

安慶
Anqing

太湖
Lake Taihu

武漢
Wuhan

九江
Jiujiang

鄱陽湖
Lake Poyang

▲上海市 Shanghai

▲黄山 Mt. Huangshan

▲南京中山陵 Sun Yetsen Mausoleum in Nanjing

編　　委/ 王國耀　但漢然　戴金象　蔡　驅
　　　　　戚永安　劉秀庭　張興定　李永暉
　　　　　施友義　黃福坤
主　　編/ 施友義
副 主 編/ 黃福坤
攝　　影/（以姓氏筆劃爲序）
　　　　　王洪柳　王富弟　朱　浩　牟航遠
　　　　　汪傳樹　李顯榮　何懷強　武永發
　　　　　祝雲清　陳　錦　陳池春　陶懋元
　　　　　梁希毅　戚永安　張宏開　張問漁
　　　　　黃加法　黃尚建　黃福坤　葉建成
　　　　　費叢高　喬德炳　楊大武　解特利
　　　　　趙貴林　熊源美　嚴越培　蘇　揚
　　　　　蘇　琳
撰　　文/ 熊源美
英　　譯/ 李榮寶　王　晶
文字編輯/ 胡　強
責任編輯/ 黃福坤
裝幀設計/ 黃福坤
封面題字/ 吳迺光

Editorial Board:	Wang Guoyao　Dan Hanran　Dai Jinxiang
	Cai Qu　Qi Yongan　Liu Xiuting
	Zhang Xingding　Li Yonghui　Shi Youyi
	Huang Fukun
Chief Editor:	Shi Youyi
Deputy Chief Editor:	Huang Fukun
Photographers:	Wang Hongliu　Wang Fudi　Zhu Hao
	Mou Hangyuan　Wang Chuanshu　Li Xianrong
	He Huaiqiang　Wu Yongfa　Zhu Yunqing
	Chen Jin　Chen Chichun　Tao Maoyuan
	Liang Xiyi　Qi Yongan　Zhang Hongkai
	Zhang Wenyu　Huang Jiafa　Huang Shangjian
	Huang Fukun　Ye Jiancheng　Fei Conggao
	Qiao Debing　Yang Dawu　Xie Teli
	Zhao Guilin　Xiong Yuanmei　Yan Yuepei
	Su Yang　Su Lin
Text by:	Xiong Yuanmei
Translators:	Li Ringbao　Wang Jing
Text Editor:	Hu Qiang
Responsible Editor:	Huang Fukun
Layout Designer:	Huang Fukun
Coverinscription by:	Wu Naiguang

長 江 三 峽
THE THREE GORGES ON
THE YANGTZE RIVER

*

出版/海風出版社

Published by Haifeng Publishing House

制版印刷/福建彩色印刷有限公司

Printed by Fujian Colour Printing Co., Ltd.

開本/889×1194　1/16　7 印張

Format: 889×1194

1994 年 5 月第一版第一次印刷

2001 年 5 月第一版第二次印刷

The First Impression of the First Edition May. 1994

ISBN 7-80597-050-5/J·25

00050　　00080